WA YEAR 12
ATAR ENGLISH
Exam Practice

Leanne Bondin
with Louise Pettigrew

insight®
innovative engaging evolving

First published in 2020, reprinted in 2020, 2021 (twice), 2022, 2023, 2024, 2025

Insight Publications Pty Ltd
3/350 Charman Road
Cheltenham Victoria 3192
Australia

Tel: +61 3 8571 4950
Email: books@insightpublications.com.au

www.insightpublications.com.au

NATIONAL LIBRARY OF AUSTRALIA

A catalogue record for this book is available from the National Library of Australia

ISBNs: 9781922378286 (print); 9781922378293 (digital)

Cover design, internal design and layout by Gisela Beer
Edited by Janice Bird
Proofread by Anica Boulanger-Mashberg
Printed by Markono Print Media Pte Ltd

Contents

INTRODUCTION

This book provides a comprehensive collection of Year 12 ATAR English examination practice questions based on the syllabus for Units 3 and 4. Each practice question is accompanied by three activities with suggested working times of 10, 20/30 and 60 minutes, including one that reflects the sort of task likely to appear in the examination. Activities have been designed to help students to develop skills that are essential to successful examination performance, such as effective annotation of texts, decoding of questions, planning, writing well within time constraints and identifying appropriate textual evidence. The book also contains tips for preparing for each section of the exam and hints that address the possible pitfalls of questions. In total, the book provides 50 different exam-style questions and more than 100 supplementary activities.

For students

The sample examination questions and the activities that accompany each question allow you to practise the skills that you will need to demonstrate in your Year 12 ATAR English exam, including important thinking and planning processes. This text should be used alongside other valuable resources, including past ATAR examinations, marking keys and examination reports available at https://www.scsa.wa.edu.au. The all-important ATAR English syllabus should be your central guiding document for preparing for the exam. In addition to all of your hard work throughout the year, completing the questions and activities in this book will ensure that you are as well prepared as you possibly can be for your Year 12 ATAR English examination – we wish you all the very best for it!

For teachers

As ATAR English teachers ourselves, we fully appreciate just how time-consuming and challenging it can be to source stimulus texts and devise practice questions in addition to those already used for class assessments. Consequently, this resource aims to support educators by providing a collection of sample questions and formative activities that promote independent student examination practice, both within the classroom and outside it. The questions and activities make for ideal lesson warm-ups, consolidation of learning, scaffolded differentiation, extension or homework tasks, and useful timed practice for all sections of the exam. This book offers many opportunities for your Year 12 students to hone and apply their understanding of the syllabus to examination-style questions, thereby equipping them with the confidence and skills critical to their success. We hope this resource becomes a valuable asset to your classroom and students.

Leanne Bondin and Louise Pettigrew

CHAPTER 1

The ATAR English Exam

This chapter provides an overview of the English examination format, as well as advice about how to effectively decode examination questions, how to plan responses and how to thoroughly prepare for the examination.

EXAM FORMAT

Reading time: 10 minutes
Writing time: three hours

SECTION	NUMBER OF QUESTIONS	NUMBER OF QUESTIONS TO ANSWER	WEIGHTING %	SUGGESTED WORKING TIME
One: Comprehending	2	2	30%	60 minutes
Two: Responding	6	1	40%	60 minutes
Three: Composing	4 or 5	1	30%	60 minutes

Section One: Comprehending

- This section is worth 30% of the total exam. The two compulsory questions are equally weighted at 15% each.
- The questions in this section require you to comprehend and analyse unseen written and visual texts.
- This section will contain two unseen texts. At least one question will require you to respond to a written text. The second text will be written, visual or multimodal.
- A question requiring you to compare the unseen texts may be included.
- Each question requires you to respond concisely in approximately 200–300 words.

Section Two: Responding

- This section is worth 40% of the total exam. It requires you to answer one question from a choice of six.
- This section requires you to demonstrate your analytical and critical thinking skills in relation to your studied text/s.
- Questions may require you to interpret, analyse, compare, contrast, reflect on and/or evaluate aspects of your studied text/s.

Section Three: Composing

- This section is worth 30% of the total exam.
- This section requires you to demonstrate your writing skills by creating a text in a particular form for a specific purpose, context and audience.
- In this section, you will answer one question from a choice of four or five. You are required to create a sustained imaginative, interpretive or persuasive text.

DECODING THE QUESTIONS

In order to successfully address a question and develop a well-structured, relevant response to it, you first need to spend time decoding and unpacking its key components. As part of your exam preparation, you should regularly practise this decoding process because it will encourage you to think critically about the questions and help to prevent any misunderstanding or misreading of them. Successful decoding of examination questions is the first step to producing high-quality responses. The table below highlights the key components – or the main word types – you should search for when deconstructing the questions in the exam.

Command words	These are the instructional terms that indicate the type of argument or response you need to write. For example, the term 'discuss' requires you to examine various aspects of a topic and provide supporting points, whereas the term 'evaluate' requires you to provide a critical judgement or appraisal.
Concept words	These refer to the important syllabus concepts that you are required to address. You need to demonstrate a deep understanding of these syllabus concepts, with reference to both your studied texts and unseen texts, as well as applying them practically through writing your own texts.
Condition words	These outline the parameters of your response, such as guiding you to apply a question to 'at least one studied text' or 'texts from the same genre'. Take careful note of condition words. Overlooking them can negatively affect your response.
Critical words	These are clarifying additional terms that make the questions more specific and nuanced, allowing markers to differentiate between candidate responses. Examples include qualifying words such as a 'particular' audience or a 'controversial' idea.

Command words

Command words are often used at the start of questions to provide a clear directive about the specific skill you need to demonstrate in your answer. To decode questions properly, you will need to understand how the command words differ from each other, sometimes very subtly. A glossary that contains these terms is available at https://senior-secondary.scsa.wa.edu.au/__data/assets/pdf_file/0006/348549/Glossary-of-key-words-used-in-the-formulation-of-questions.pdf. The table below summarises some common command words that you may encounter in English examination questions.

Command	What you need to do
Account for	Provide reasons or justifications
Analyse	Identify the components; explain their relationship, function and effects
Compare	Identify points of similarity and difference
Create	Make, craft or compose
Discuss	Examine the various aspects; provide supporting points
Evaluate	Critically appraise or provide a judgement
Explain	Identify the why and/or how of something through a focus on cause and effect
Explore	Thoroughly investigate or search for
Identify	Recognise and label or name specifically

Sample decoded questions

Observe these worked examples, which highlight how you might decode the different types of questions in the Comprehending, Responding or Composing sections of the exam.

Sample Section One question: Comprehending

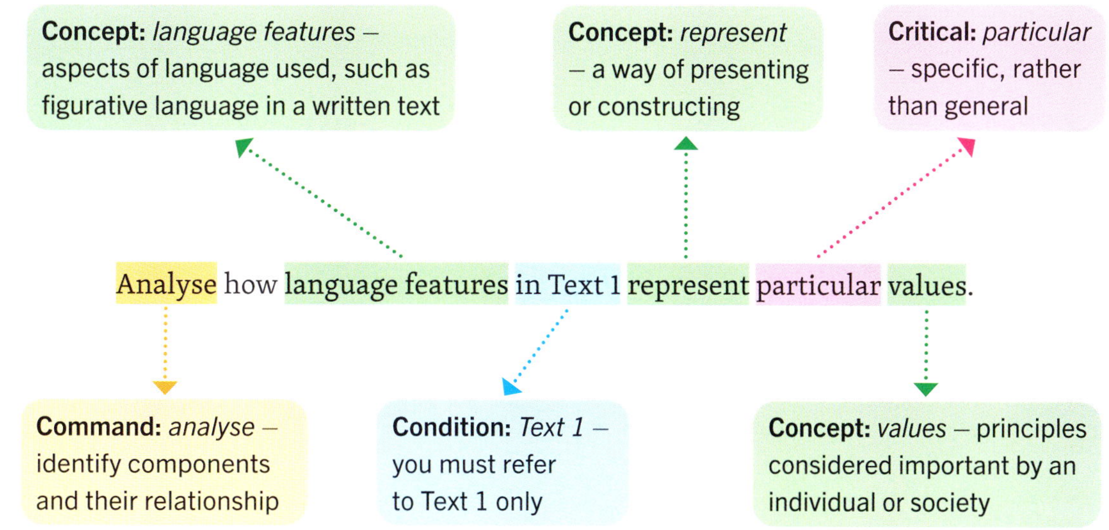

Sample Section Two question: Responding

Command: *evaluate* – make a critical judgement

Critical: *impact* – the effect

Critical: *author's choice* – implies purposeful deliberation

Condition: *at least one text you have studied* – choice of one or more studied texts

Evaluate the impact of an author's choice of language features on your response to at least one text you have studied.

Concept: *language features* – aspects of language used, e.g. figurative language (in a written text) or camera shots, music and dialogue (in a multimodal text)

Concept: *your response* – your reaction, feeling as the reader/viewer; invites use of pronoun 'I'

Sample Section Three question: Composing

Command: *create* – write or compose

Condition: *a text* – just one text

Critical: *manipulates* – not simply 'uses' – controls purposefully, adjusts, may challenge convention

Create a text that manipulates textual features for a particular effect.

Concept: *textual features* – any language, generic, stylistic or structural features of the text

Critical: *particular* – specific, rather than general

Concept: *effect* – a specific impact; the way in which meaning is shaped

APPROACHES TO PLANNING

Once you have decoded the key words and phrases of a question, you then need to plan your response to it. Although plans are not considered to be part of a response and therefore don't directly earn marks, developing a plan before you begin writing your answer is critically important. Taking time to plan will enable you to consider all aspects of a question, clarify your thoughts, order your response logically, and build a strong framework for your response. Think of your plan as being like a road map, setting out the direction of your response and orienting you so that you have a clear sense of exactly where you intend to go. If you have a mental block or lose your train of thought during the writing process, referring to your plan will help you get back on track.

Plans need only be brief and can take multiple forms, including the following.

- **Brief dot points written directly around, above or underneath a question** on the examination paper itself. This way, you can ensure that you are considering each word in turn and not accidentally overlooking any.
- **A list of ideas**, such as the main focus for each paragraph. Some students also like to record in their plans the quotes they intend to use in their responses.
- **A thesis statement or an overarching guiding statement** that summarises a response or approach to a question.
- **Brainstorming synonyms for the key words of the question** to enhance understanding of it. Some students find it useful to extend this process to rewriting the question in their own words.
- **Colour-coding or numbering** parts of a question and the corresponding parts in the unseen text (Comprehending section).
- **A narrative plot diagram** indicating the significant moments of development or a character profile (Composing section).
- **A list of points corresponding to acronyms or mnemonics** such as CAPs or GAPPS (Composing section) – see the next page for an explanation of these terms.

Consider the strategies suggested in the table on the next page as possible ways to plan for each section of the examination. Given the time constraints of the exam, it is advisable to allocate a specific amount of time for planning in each section – about five minutes per question is usually a good target.

Section One: Comprehending 60 minutes	• Decode each question carefully, taking note of its different word types and the specific syllabus concepts or examinable content it is seeking to assess. • Read the question before the unseen text, to narrow your analytical focus. • Carefully read the contextual information that accompanies each text, to help you predict its textual features, ideas or subject matter. • Spend a few minutes annotating each text and pinpointing the key aspects related to the question. • Briefly make planning notes around or directly underneath/above the question, in dot-point form.

Section Two: Responding 60 minutes	• Decode the selected question carefully, taking note of its word types and the specific syllabus concepts or examinable content it is seeking to assess.
	• Consider planning the following for your selected question:
	  ○ a thesis statement
	  ○ three or four supporting points
	  ○ evidence, quotes and textual examples.
	• Plans can also take the form of a brainstorm, a mind map, a topic sentence for each paragraph, a list in dot points or another type of diagram.

Section Three: Composing 60 minutes	• Decode the selected question carefully, taking note of its word types and the specific syllabus concepts or examinable content it is seeking to assess. • Decide on the following aspects of your response during planning: Context, Audience, Purpose (CAP) – write a dot point or two under each heading as a plan. • Alternatively, decide how you will fill in the GAPPS for the reader (Genre/Form, Audience, Purpose, Persona, Situational context) – write a dot point or two under each heading. (Note that the GAPPS method of planning is particularly suited to interpretive or persuasive responses.) • Draft a title which will orient the reader by revealing important information about your response, such as its genre, form, subject matter, audience and intended situational context. • Plans can also take the form of a brainstorm, a mind map, a list in dot points, a plot overview, a character profile etc.

DESIGNING YOUR OWN QUESTIONS

Designing your own examination questions is a very effective way to practise for the examination. While the types of questions in each section of the exam may look slightly different from one another, they all have a common grounding in the examinable content of Units 3 and 4, which you also need to use in your own design of practice questions. The specific types of questions you can expect in each section are covered in the following chapters. In designing your own practice examination questions, experiment with the following three strategies.

1 Compile a list, or create a table like the one below, to record terms typical of each word type. Mix and match a selection from this list to design your own questions.

Command words	Concept words	Condition words	Critical words
analyse evaluate compare	voice perspective values	at least one text a text two texts	empathy for *a group* *controversial* idea manipulates

Design a practice question in this space which uses one word or phrase from each column above.

2 Transform the syllabus examinable content into practice questions.

Copy one of the bullet points from the examinable content of the syllabus into this space. • e.g. Evaluate different perspectives, attitudes and values represented in texts by *exploring other interpretations and aspects of context to develop a considered response*.
Now design a practice question that rearranges the syntax but retains the main concepts contained within this bullet point. e.g. Evaluate the extent to which your response to a text has been influenced by an understanding of the contextual factors that have shaped its representations.

3 Change the syllabus concepts in questions from previous exams.

In the space below, copy a question from a previous ATAR exam (available at https://senior-secondary.scsa.wa.edu.au).
Now design a practice question that replaces the syllabus concepts with different ones.

REVISING AND PREPARING

English revision is most effective when it is done consistently across your units of work – rather than at the last minute before an exam – and when it employs a wide range of strategies. The following suggestions will help you to achieve this breadth of approach and will enhance your preparation for the exam. Place a tick in the box beside each strategy as you implement it.

English revision and preparation strategies	
◯	**Revise your selected texts according to the concepts of the course syllabus.** Devise a checklist of syllabus concepts and apply them to practice analyses of your studied texts.
◯	**Create succinct summaries of your studied texts' themes, ideas, issues and concepts.** Link these to language features and patterns, stylistic and structural features, genre etc.
◯	**Select key quotations or textual evidence to memorise from your studied texts.** Make sure they can be connected to multiple syllabus concepts and points of examinable content.
◯	**Compare your studied texts.** Create Venn diagrams and comparison tables to note the similarities and differences between at least two studied texts.
◯	**Revise key scenes or moments.** Take your analysis of a specific scene (in a film or a written narrative) and try to adapt it so that it focuses on a different concept, such as conventions, mode or structure.
◯	**Expand your vocabulary.** Learn one new word or metalanguage term per day or week. Download a word-a-day app or create a metalanguage word-wall in your bedroom.
◯	**Create flashcards and posters defining syllabus concepts.** Use definitions in the course glossary and put them in prominent places around your bedroom so you are immersed in the language of the syllabus.
◯	**Create visual summaries.** Draw colour-coded mind maps or flow charts of key moments in one or more studied text/s. Keep them visible in the room where you study.
◯	**Form a study group or book club with friends.** Discuss studied texts or wider reading with peers and friends, edit each other's work and design quizzes to test your collective knowledge.
◯	**Practise your handwriting skills.** Writing by hand in the exam for three hours straight can be challenging so it is a skill that needs to be practised regularly.
◯	**Source your own extracts for Section One.** Seek out various forms, including satirical cartoons, graphic novel pages, open letters, editorials, diary entries, blog posts, webpages and infographics.
◯	**Read, and view, widely.** Read around topics you have studied in class. Watch and read reputable sources of news (on TV, online and in print) to keep up to date with current affairs and issues.

◯	**Complete practice under both open book and timed conditions.** Refer to your notes and studied text/s initially, then work without them, before gradually reducing the time you allow yourself to complete responses.
◯	**Practise responding to questions from past exams.** The practice questions in this book should be used to supplement those from past exams on the SCSA website.
◯	**Design your own questions.** This will develop your understanding of the syllabus, build your confidence and familiarise you with what to expect of the questions in the exam.
◯	**Design your own marking guides.** Follow the examples in this book or marking keys used for past exams; adopting the mindset of a marker will allow you to consider what is being rewarded in responses.
◯	**Practise thinking and planning.** You don't always need to produce full answers when revising or practising. Spend 10 minutes every day thinking about a question and producing just a plan or just a thesis statement.
◯	**Edit, rewrite and resubmit previous responses for feedback.** Submit these to your teacher and politely request feedback, or conduct peer reviews.
◯	**Collect exemplars of good responses from each section of the exam.** Ask your teacher to show you some of the best responses to previous assessments and exams, as exemplars to aim for.
◯	**Familiarise yourself with past examination reports.** These documents, published on the SCSA website, summarise important comments and highlight common errors and pitfalls.

TIME MANAGEMENT IN THE EXAM

Managing your time in the examination is imperative to your overall success. Keep in mind the following points.

- The 10-minute reading time can be used to get an overall impression of the exam. As the front cover is released to schools prior to the exam, you should only need to give this a quick scan.
- Once you have read all of the questions in section order, return to the unseen texts in the Comprehending section to begin a closer reading.
- Use a clock or countdown recorded by exam invigilators in the room to monitor the time. Some candidates find it useful to write on the exam paper the time at which they will need to finish each section. There is never a reason to finish an exam early; any extra time should be used for proofreading and improving your responses. Spend **approximately** the following amount of time working on each section.

Comprehending	Responding	Composing
8–10 minutes for reading, annotating and planning per text/question	5 minutes planning	5 minutes planning
18–20 minutes writing per question	50 minutes writing	50 minutes writing
2–3 minutes proofreading each question	5 minutes proofreading	5 minutes proofreading

- Under time pressure, you may be tempted to skip an essential step like planning. Always plan! It is the only way to organise your thoughts properly.
- The exam sections are placed in their particular order for good reason – as the unseen texts in Section One will be fresh in your minds after the 10-minute reading time, it makes sense to start with this section. It is appropriate that the Composing section is placed last because it requires different skills and writing styles from Sections One and Two, and involves constructing a text rather than deconstructing it.
- While the previous point is important, some candidates do achieve success working through the sections in a different order. However, unless you have practised extensively and enjoyed success with an alternative sequence in past semester exams, you should follow the section order in the external ATAR exam.
- A time recommendation is given for each section of the exam. While you might sacrifice time from one section to give to another, this can be risky, and should be limited to a maximum of 10 minutes. Again, only use this approach if it has proved successful in your school-based exams.
- The best way to conquer time-management issues is with consistent timed practice.
- DO NOT make the mistake of spending excessive time writing an overly long response for Section Two, just because it is worth more than the other sections. Depth of analysis is *always* preferable over length – quality over quantity. Quality analysis is achieved by engaging closely with the question and selecting supporting evidence discerningly.

Note that presentation of material in the following chapters occasionally differs slightly from its presentation in the exam.

- For some of the practice activities in Chapter 2, two texts are presented on a single page to allow for ease of comparison. An alphabetical letter qualification – A or B – is provided for each text to allow you to distinguish between them in your responses. In the exam, texts to be compared are typically placed on separate pages and labelled Text 1, Text 2 etc.
- Some texts in Chapter 2 are presented in columns; however, texts in the exam typically run across the page.
- Some stimulus images in Chapter 4 are presented in colour; however, the exam is produced in black and white.

Comprehending Practice

CHAPTER 2

This chapter addresses the demands of Section One of the examination. It includes 20 different practice questions focused on the comprehension and analysis of a wide range of written, visual and multimodal texts. A working time of 30 minutes is recommended for each of these questions. This reflects the demands of Section One, in which two questions need to be answered in a suggested 60-minute time frame. In addition to these Comprehending section practice questions, this chapter includes the following.

- A 10-minute activity accompanying each practice question provides scaffolded support to help you decode the question, annotate and deconstruct the text purposefully, enhance comprehension of the text and plan a response.
- A 60-minute activity accompanying each practice question generally provides the opportunity to reflect on, edit and improve your responses to the practice questions. These activities are sometimes designed around using the texts as models and stimuli for your own writing, helping you to develop skills transferable to other sections of the examination.
- Brief 'handy hints' accompany some questions that might present particular pitfalls; the hints will direct you away from potential misreadings of the questions.

WHAT TO EXPECT IN SECTION ONE

This is what you can expect to encounter in the Comprehending section.

- You will need to demonstrate a very close reading of the unseen texts. The questions usually have a narrow, targeted analytical focus on the syllabus examinable content.
- You will almost certainly be asked to write responses to texts that you have not studied, or in forms that may not have appeared in previous exams. With the exception of poetry or drama, the texts could include almost any kind of written, visual or multimodal text.

- Although it is highly likely that the specific texts in the exam will be unfamiliar, you will still be able to draw on your prior experience of other texts that belong to a similar form, genre, context etc. The exam texts may use language, structural, generic or stylistic features that you *do* recognise.
- Try to use personal pronouns such as 'I' or 'me' in your analysis if the question invites you to. Questions in past exams have required an explanation of how a text may engage 'you' or how 'your' response or interpretation has been shaped.
- The texts will probably be multilayered and nuanced in their ideas; there are likely to be many possible 'correct' answers to each question.
- Remember that each analysis in this section needs to be concise, at only 200–300 words. For most students, this equates to just over a page of writing.

TYPES OF QUESTIONS IN SECTION ONE

Section One requires you to provide very close analysis of the unseen texts. The Comprehending questions can be quite short, assessing your understanding of just one or two key syllabus concepts. An understanding of the relationship *between* the concepts may be of critical importance to answering a question properly. The questions typically start with a command word, such as 'analyse' or explain', followed by 'how', indicating that answers should be firmly grounded in analysis that explains the workings of the text. The questions might be quite 'open' in nature, allowing you to discuss your personal interpretation of a text and to select whatever features you like to support it. Or they might be more 'closed', with condition or critical words directing you to focus on a specific idea or one aspect of construction, for instance. Definitions of 'command', 'concept', 'condition' and 'critical' are explained on page 2.

Example Comprehending question

Explain how Text 1 is constructed to communicate an idea about youth in Australia.

The most important considerations for the types of questions in this section are:

- understanding that, because of their brevity, *all* the words they contain are important
- being able to identify the specific syllabus concepts being assessed
- recognising the relationship *between* the syllabus concepts being assessed.

The types of questions included in this section may require you to:

- deconstruct the text carefully at the word or micro level, much like examining it through the lens of a magnifying glass
- direct your attention away from what you may *want* to analyse, through the specificity of the wording
- compare and/or contrast the unseen texts
- reflect on your response/s to a text
- justify your interpretation/s of a text
- demonstrate an understanding of visual and written language features
- recognise subtleties, nuanced meanings and juxtaposition within the texts
- select appropriate quotes and textual evidence in order to support your argument
- use metalanguage appropriate to the form and mode of the text.

TOP TIPS FOR SECTION ONE

The following tips offer advice for achieving success in Section One.

- Use the 10-minute reading time to establish an overall sense of the texts. Then, in the working time, devote 30 minutes to each question. Read the question first, then the contextual information provided, then the text. The contextual information often provides vital clues about the text, allowing you to develop helpful expectations of its subject matter, conventions or techniques.
- Deconstruct the questions carefully. Identify the command, concept, condition and critical words. Identify the relationship between any syllabus concepts.
- Plan! This process is critical in terms of focusing your thoughts and providing you with a clear framework. A plan only needs to be brief. In this section it might consist of a few dot points around or above the question itself.
- Start with a clear thesis that engages specifically with *all* aspects of the question. No general statements should be provided in this section; get straight to the point! You can reiterate the thesis at the end of your response with a sentence that relates back to the question, using different words or syntax.
- Annotate the texts, focusing *only* on what is important to answering the question. Avoid simply highlighting the text. Rather, label, number or colour-code parts of the text that could be used as textual evidence.
- Embed quotes and evidence smoothly, and do not plagiarise the writer's work. Quotes should be short; sometimes paraphrasing is just as effective.
- Comprehending responses don't need to resemble 'mini-essays'. The questions usually lend themselves to short answers of one to three paragraphs – only use a paragraph break if shifting focus significantly. A separate introduction and conclusion are unnecessary.

PRACTICE QUESTIONS AND ACTIVITIES

This section contains a variety of sample texts, with associated practice questions and activities to develop your skills.

Text 1

The following extract is from a 2018 novel titled *Dustfall*, by Western Australian author Michelle Johnston.

When a building dies it cracks open, and new life drifts in on breezes and seeds. A resurrection, blown in from elsewhere. Or perhaps more a rebirth, Lou thinks, reserved solely for things of bricks and mortar, for the never-lived. Not for people, that's for sure. Certainly, not for the little one with the jiggle in her step and the smell of unwashed clothes. No, when humans die they crumble into dust with barely a whisper, and are poured into urns for display on mute mantelpieces, or shelved away silently underground, leaving nothing but official paperwork and vast, endless wreckage.

Lou looks up to the craterous holes in the walls, the yawning openings, where these motes, inklings really, waft in from who knows where. The specks float to the floor without sound, looking like snow, except it's hot. Hotter than she's ever known it, which is something, considering she comes from Perth, a city as baked and dry as forgotten bread.

The hospital is a ruin, without plaque or monument, marked only by a broken *Keep Out* sign, its face canting and creaking on the haunt of a wind, and an entrance flanked by listing pillars that she fancies look like fractured, crippled metacarpals.

Sitting propped up against a half-standing wall, the warmth soaks through her shirt, and the edges of bricks jut on angles into her back. Many of the walls have disintegrated entirely, leaving drifts of grey concrete crumbs which have settled into layers all the way through the building, writing down the story of the place; a chronicle that no one's around to read.

It must have been a large room, this central one. In a corner is a steel contraption, all rusted cylinders and curved pipes. An anaesthetic machine, she guesses, now just a relic – nothing like the modern ones she's been recently spinning the dials of, dispensing their lolly-like vapours of oblivion to the lucky ones under the mask. Lou hauls herself up, wiping her muddy hands on her pants, and walks towards it. She rubs the front of her wrist over one of the canisters. An asinine gesture, she thinks, as if a genie might appear and extinguish this whole episode on the wave of command. A hint of shine emerges – peculiar, after all these years.

On the floor nearby is a bundle of papers, covered in layers of dried muck. She squats next to it and picks off several clods. The top one is an Australian medical journal, dated from sometime in the fifties, although it's difficult to make out the bleached, rippled words. Amazing that they are here, as if waiting patiently to be read.

Picking up the paper by its corner, it perishes with a puff, filling the air with the smell of gunpowder. Lying underneath is an envelope, eaten through by the hunger of years and the climate. The writing that remains is faded and barely visible – she can just distinguish an elaborate, looping scrawl. She tries to lift it, but when she does, it also crumbles in her hand, the pieces drifting away like word pollen. Lost to the breeze. Gone. She imagines doing the same herself, dissolving on a breath of air and joining the backlit diaspora.

Comprehending Practice Question 1

Analyse the relationship between setting and character in Text 1.

HANDY HINT The word 'relationship' invites you to consider the way the setting impacts or influences the character, the way the character relates to or interacts with their environment, the character's response to the setting etc.

ACTIVITIES

10-minute activity

a Carefully annotate Text 1 in its margins, using the analytical focus of Comprehending Practice Question 1.

b Create an opening thesis statement addressing each part of the question.

___

___

___

30-minute activity

Respond concisely to Comprehending Practice Question 1 in approximately 200–300 words.

60-minute activity

a Write a complete response to Comprehending Practice Question 1.

b Carefully compare your response to the points made in the Sample Marking Guide provided on pages 93–4.

c Use the information contained in the marking guide to edit and improve your response.

Text 2

The following text is a black-and-white photograph by Stuart Franklin captioned 'Manchester. Moss Side Estate.' It was taken on a council estate in the United Kingdom in 1986, during a time of widespread unemployment.

Comprehending Practice Question 2

Explain how Text 2 conveys the experience of being a child.

10-minute activity

Annotate Text 2 and complete the table below, selecting the most significant visual elements used to convey the experience of being a child.

Visual elements (e.g. body language, composition, proxemics)	Use adjectives to describe the experience of being a child as conveyed in the text

30-minute activity

Respond concisely to Comprehending Practice Question 2 in approximately 200–300 words.

60-minute activity

a Find a black-and-white photograph (online or in a magazine/newspaper) that captures a different setting to that of Text 2 (e.g. a natural landscape, a domestic interior).

b Using Text 2 and your additional selected text, respond to the following question in approximately 200–300 words.

Compare how the texts represent different settings through aspects of their construction.

c Highlight the 'compare' and 'contrast' terminology in your response (e.g. likewise, similarly, by contrast, both, on the other hand).

Text 3

The following extract is from an article written by Zachary Bruce. It was published on the ABC News website in 2020.

WA town of Ballidu is 'doing its own thing' with contemporary art

It looks like the set of a Wes Anderson film with the streets lined with quirky sculptures and kitsch buildings painted in whimsical pastel hues.

Nude portraits adorn the walls of the local drinking hole, but it's not the questionable content you would expect to find in a country pub.

Arriving at Ballidu, just over 200 kilometres north-east of Perth, feels more like delving into a living art installation than a farming town of around 70 people.

In the 1990s the tiny town attracted kooky characters from across the country, hosting visual artists who were riding the wave of increased arts funding.

They helped transform the quiet wheat-farming village into a visual feast.

But in the past decade, those art residencies have evaporated.

Painter and co-founder of the Ballidu Lodge Art Gallery Pamella Toster said a change to the public funding of the arts had most likely contributed to the downturn.

"The funding has gone; I think things are a little bit harder. They [artists] need to work and earn money and they can't get away," she said.

"The 90s were a time of government support of the arts, really trying to get it out there and push it along a bit, and there was federal and state funding for that."

When the visiting artists stopped coming residents began to rely on their own art practice to quench their thirst for contemporary art.

"We've got this little group that has got together and said 'we want to do our own thing; we want to be as good as we can'," Ms Toster said.

"We're sort of inspiring each other ... that's a really new thing for us ... because the original idea was to bring the contemporary arts to our rural community because there was nothing like that here."

Ballidu Tavern manager John Gould is one of the artists flourishing in the local art renaissance; his pub is packed with nude portraits of Ballidu residents.

He said Pamella inspired him to try his hand at drawing.

"One night, when she'd had a couple of ports too many, she was asking a painter, signwriter, if he'd do a picture of her nude."

He said that was the moment he decided to take up sketching.

"The locals seemed to get on board quite readily after I had done a couple of pictures," he said.

"They were more or less lining up for me to add their portrait to figures I've got around the pub."

Mr Gould said he was making up for lost time, after a childhood where boys were expected to do woodwork and drafting, while the girls were encouraged to take up art.

Comprehending Practice Question 3

Provide reasons why the stylistic features of Text 3 shape your response to it.

HANDY HINT The question is only concerned with **your** personal response to the text so use pronouns such as 'I' and 'me' rather than objective terms like 'the audience'.

10-minute activity

In the space below copy the definition of 'stylistic features' provided in the course glossary.

____

____

____

____

____

____

On Text 3, highlight and label evidence of its stylistic features. List three of these stylistic features below.

Stylistic feature 1: ______________________________

Stylistic feature 2: ______________________________

Stylistic feature 3: ______________________________

30-minute activity

Respond concisely to Comprehending Practice Question 3 in approximately 200–300 words.

60-minute activity

Design a detailed marking guide suitable for Comprehending Practice Question 3. Use the example provided on pages 93–4 as a model.

Text 4

The following image is a greyscale version of an advertisement for a watch brand.

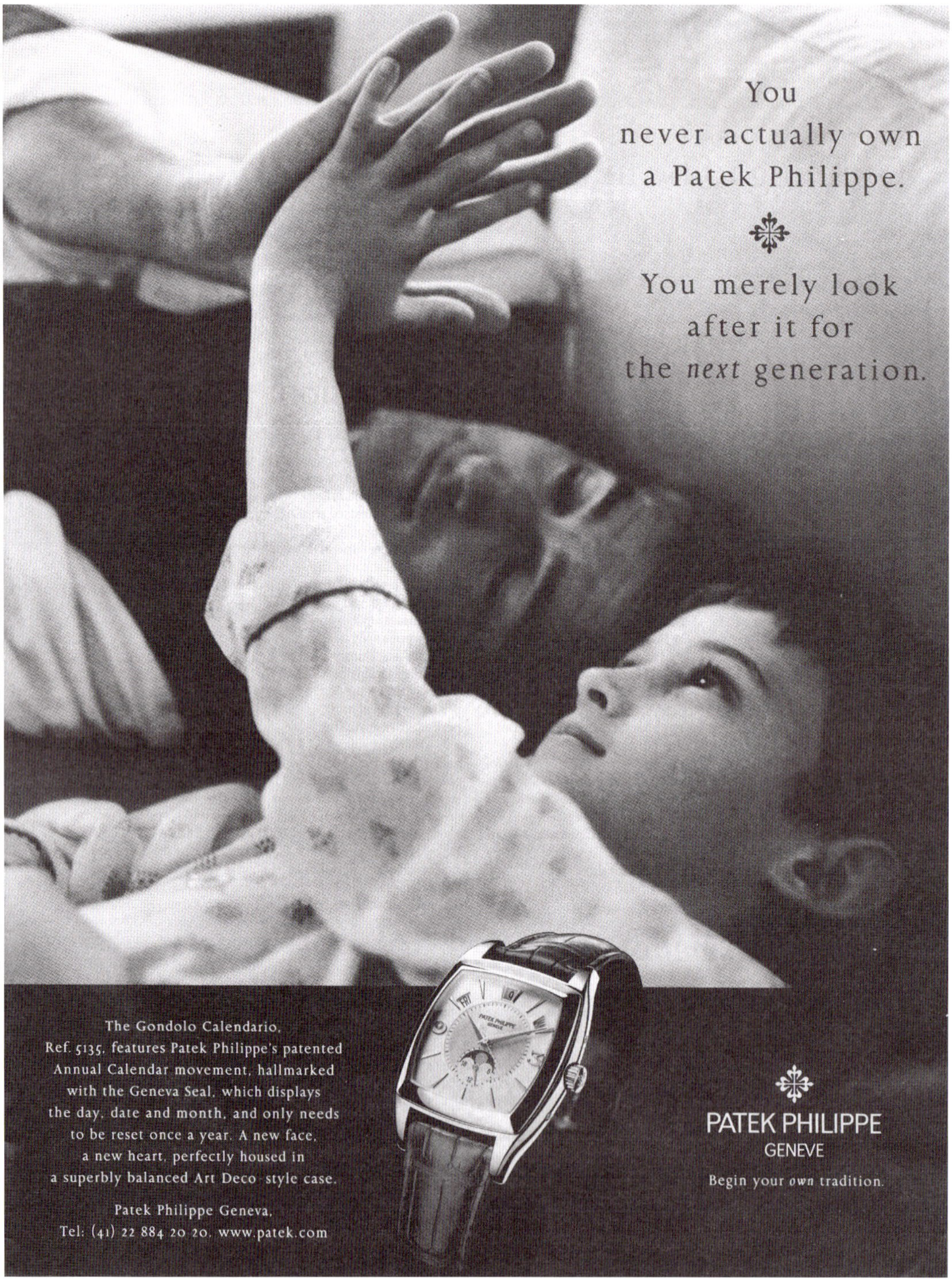

Comprehending Practice Question 4

Analyse the way in which written and visual features in Text 4 are used to appeal to the values of an audience.

HANDY HINT Remember to specifically identify the likely audience of the text. Also note the plural 'values', meaning you need to identify at least two of them.

10-minute activity

Annotate the text in its margins, then complete the following table.

Visual/written feature	Which value is appealed to? Why?
Audience demographic (consider age, gender, societal and cultural group etc.)	

30-minute activity

Respond concisely to Comprehending Practice Question 4 in approximately 200–300 words.

60-minute activity

a Find **two** more advertisements that promote an accessory (e.g. watch, jewellery, sunglasses). You can find these in magazines or newspapers, or on websites.

b Write three short paragraphs that describe the likely audience of each advertisement. Provide evidence to support your answer.

c Explain which of the three advertisements is most successful in appealing to your own values and why.

Text 5

The following extract is from a 2020 blog by Nicole Hasham, published on *The Conversation* website.

Bushfires plunder lives and landscapes in myriad ways, but they often start the same way. A bright morning suddenly turns to night. Ash flutters down from the sky, propelled ahead of the roaring fire front. An awful red glow slinks over the horizon.

When I awoke in the NSW south coast town of Bermagui on the last day of 2019, I should have twigged straight away. At 8am the sky was a gruesome orange-black, the surrounding bush freakishly quiet. Our mobile phones had no signal. Outside, my car was coated in soot.

We knew fires were burning more than 100km up the coast at Batemans Bay, but Bermagui had seemed a safe distance away. Suddenly, it wasn't.

Fire was bearing down on the seaside town, burning so fiercely it created its own thunderstorm. Residents evacuated to the beach after emergency text messages at 4am, but with our phone service down we'd slept on, oblivious. When my partner and I woke and worked out what was happening, we too bundled our bewildered young son into the car and fled.

Of course, amid the devastation wrought this fire season, a disrupted holiday is nothing to complain about. Bushfires have decimated huge swathes of Australia this fire season, taking with them, at the time of writing, 23 lives and more than 1500 homes.

Thousands of holidaymakers in NSW and Victoria were stranded for days in towns with dwindling food and fuel supplies. Some were forced to shelter on beaches, dodging embers and watching flames creep ever closer. And we cannot forget the animals – millions have been killed this fire season, or will soon die from lack of food or shelter.

With all roads out of Bermagui closed, we spent New Year's Eve at a local club which had hastily been converted into an evacuation centre. Many evacuees were from the nearby fire-hit town of Cobargo. Some knew the father and son who died after staying to defend their property. Many would presumably soon discover their own homes were gone. They watched, hands over their mouths, as the club's giant plasma screens beamed images of their once-charming town, now a jumble of rubble and corrugated iron.

We lay our doonas down between rows of poker machines and lined up for dinner with hundreds of other evacuees. Food supplies in the town had already run short – the shelves of the local Woolworths were all but empty. To feed the hordes, volunteers began rationing dinner portions to just half a sausage and a slice of bread. They had no idea where tomorrow's meals would come from.

All this raises inevitable questions. To what extent is climate change driving these fires, and how much of that is Australia's fault? Do we need a permanent, paid rural fire-fighting force to deal with this "new normal"? Are our fuel, food and communications systems resilient enough to cope with these disasters? And how do we cope with the deep anxiety these fires provoke, on both a personal and societal level?

Comprehending Practice Question 5

Explain how Text 5 offers an interpretation of the bushfires.

HANDY HINT Be careful not to invert the question to explain *your* interpretation of the bushfires; the focus needs to be on the way *the author* offers their interpretation of it through aspects of the text's construction.

ACTIVITIES

10-minute activity

Locate examples of the following techniques used in Text 5. Record each example as a short quote in the table below.

Technique	Quote from the text
Alliteration	
Connotative verb	
Emotive language	
Inclusive diction	
Rhetorical question	
Statistic	

30-minute activity

Respond concisely to Comprehending Practice Question 5 in approximately 200–300 words.

60-minute activity

Transform the content of the article into one of the following forms:

- a personal letter
- an interview transcript
- a diary entry

Ensure that you use the conventions of the form you have selected to write in.

Texts 6A and 6B

Text 6A is an extract from the short story 'Purple Little Hearts' by Perth-based writer and teacher EL Marriott. Text 6B is a page from the graphic novel *Black Hole* by Charles Burns, which explores the transition from adolescence to adulthood.

Text 6A

Slowly, he retracted from my limp embrace and faded into the thin washed-out walls of an old building built for the disenfranchised. A hospital gown loosely tied at the small of his back painted a sorry vision of him; one I did not want to remember but could never forget. He stacked the empty drawers one by one on the hospital bed as if it were a paid task. His actions made no sense. Watching him, it was as if a cloud appeared above me and rained all of its misty contents over me. How would I change the weather now?

I cast my mind back to one overcast day, where a wet lilac sky was my only companion in searching the dirty city streets for him. Fear and desperation punctuated the journey, the shortness of my breath and the tingling in my fingertips intensifying as I turned each corner. I knew that boy, Danny, he was hanging around with was trouble. But I never imagined this: a seven-day drug-induced bender that threw all he had into the overflowing dumpster where I finally found him. When I peered inside, we were all in there too: mum, dad, nana and Scruffy our dog. His life of addiction poisoned our lives. These six years were now unbearable and a time which overshadowed this town. Those who were tempted became lost, forgotten members of society. I was not one of them, but I was tired of making it my mission to clean up the mess.

As I turned to leave, I caught my reflection in the old mirror above the sink and in that moment I was lost and found. I had a choice to make. Was this who I was now – a junkie's carer? I grabbed my bag and headed out the door, to finally leave it all behind.

Text 6B

Comprehending Practice Question 6

Compare how Texts A and B explore a similar emotion.

HANDY HINT

The command word 'compare' clearly indicates you should look at similarities and differences between the texts. Look at contrasts between the ways they are constructed because of their different modes or forms.

ACTIVITIES

10-minute activity

Read Texts 6A and 6B, then complete the Venn diagram below.

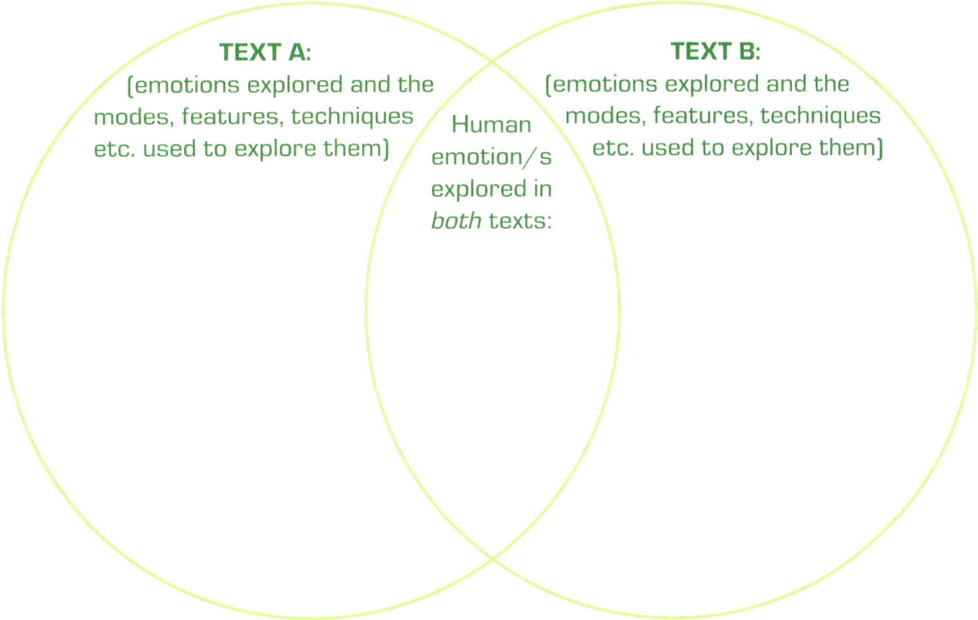

30-minute activity

Respond concisely to Comprehending Practice Question 6 in approximately 200–300 words.

60-minute activity

Find a *visual* image that explores an idea or subject matter similar to that in one of your studied *written* texts. Respond, in the form of an analytical essay, to the following question.

Compare how your studied text and the selected image explore similar ideas or subject matter despite their contrasting modes.

Text 7

The following text is an image by Perth photographer Dan Nelson. It was taken in India in 2013.

Comprehending Practice Question 7

Evaluate which visual elements work most effectively to depict these people as having a sense of purpose.

ACTIVITIES

10-minute activity

a In the space below, brainstorm a list of visual elements evident in Text 7.

____

____

____

____

____

b Now circle the *two* visual elements that you believe are the most effective in depicting the people in the image as having a sense of purpose.

c Briefly discuss and compare your choices with a peer. Justify why you each believe your personal selections are the most effective in depicting the people's sense of purpose.

30-minute activity

Respond concisely to Comprehending Practice Question 7 in approximately 200–300 words.

60-minute activity

a Complete the 30-minute activity above.

b Carefully proofread and edit your response.

c Type your response, making improvements and modifications where necessary.

d Now compare your response with that of a peer from your class or study group. Discuss with them the:

- similarities between your responses
- differences between your responses
- reasons for developing different responses to the text.

Text 8A

The following is an extract from a chapter titled 'Disgust and enchantment' in *Island Home: A Landscape Memoir*, by Western Australian author Tim Winton.

When I was twelve my family left the suburbs of Perth and moved south to Albany. It was a radical dislocation. For a long time I was lonely and miserable and from the outset it seemed that the weather and the landscape of this new environment were conspiring to make things worse. Gone were the blue skies, the bright tutting of cicadas, the roasting consolation of the sun. I missed my friends, but I also felt the loss of home territory – the soughing dune sheoaks and dusty limestone scales of the dry sand country of the midwest. Here in the south a gothic gloom hung over the landscape. There were actual mountains in the distance. Sometimes snow whitened their peaks. Albany cowered between high rainswept tors, and the wind-torn harbour was flecked like the lips of a lunatic. Just as the local kids seemed to seethe and spoil for a bit of biff at school, the town felt like it was always about to lash out. It was dark, tamped down, sodden, but hot and unpredictable underneath, like a peaty paddock.

Text 8B

The following extract is an autobiographical reflection written by Dr David Smith, a retired Brisbane academic who moved from Durban, South Africa, 40 years ago.

Very gently, I turned aside the blanket and crept toward the porthole to peer out across the vast expanse of ocean. It had been a long and somewhat rough voyage and my wife, five months pregnant with our first child, had battled the twin hazards of morning sickness and often turbulent seas. As I drew aside the flimsy curtain, I could just make out a few faint lights on the horizon. Maybe I was seeing things that were not there. I kept looking. No, they were definitely, unmistakably lights. We would soon be able to step ashore on this vast continent that was to be my new home. I felt a warm cheek pressed against mine. "I was too excited to sleep," my wife whispered. We embraced, feelings of exhilaration coursing through us, united in a joyous shared experience.

For my Australian-born wife, stepping ashore would represent the first step towards a homecoming. For me, it held the promise of a new environment where race relations were not an all-pervasive issue. Our first steps ashore were to be the precursor of a permanent move to another country where my memories of life under apartheid could gradually be supplanted by the immediacy of life in a new country.

Yet, like an unexpected clap of thunder on a sunny day, a sudden and strange apprehension gripped me – cocooned inside the warm body huddled against my own was another being, a being who was unknowingly, helplessly, being transported to another land of our choosing where his or her life would unfold. What awesome power a parent has!

Comprehending Practice Question 8

Compare how the texts represent the experience of moving to live in a new place.

10-minute activity

Find an example of the following features in each of the texts.

Textual feature	Text A	Text B
Simile		
Alliteration		
Organic imagery		
Juxtaposition		
Tone		

30-minute activity

Respond concisely to Comprehending Practice Question 8 in approximately 200–300 words.

60-minute activity

Using the features listed in the table, compose your own piece of writing that reflects on a personal experience of moving. Your response could explore moving between cities, countries, schools, rooms or any other two locations.

Text 9

The following text is a greyscale version of a *New Scientist* magazine cover from 2015.

Comprehending Practice Question 9

Analyse how visual and written modes interact in this text to shape audience expectations.

HANDY HINT Your response could focus on any expectations generated by the visual and written features of this text, including features related to its genre, form, subject matter, multimodality etc.

10-minute activity

Find definitions and synonyms for the following words in Comprehending Practice Question 9.

Word	Definition	Synonyms
analyse		
interact		
shape		
expectations		

30-minute activity

Respond concisely to Comprehending Practice Question 9 in approximately 200–300 words.

60-minute activity

Find an example of each of the following types of multimodal texts:

- an album cover
- an infographic
- a webpage

For each of your three chosen texts, respond to Comprehending Practice Question 9 and develop an opening thesis.

Text 10

The following is an extract from an opinion piece by Peter FitzSimons, published in *The Sydney Morning Herald*.

It is time for our government to take strong action against the scourge of our times, the appalling and terrifying phenomenon that is wiping out innocents from all walks of life, devastating families and leaving lives in ruin.

I refer, of course, to ...

You thought I was going to say terrorism? Uh, no. On Australian soil – which is to say the territory the Australian government can most easily control – our country has lost fewer people to terrorism since September 11 than we lose in *a day* to the ravages of obesity-related conditions.

Last week the government announced it would be conducting a review of its Health Star Rating System on food products, which, as you know, is meant to be the official guide as to just how healthy a product is, by virtue of the number of stars it displays on the package. If it gets five out of five stars, it's top of the pops and, you'd assume, so healthy you'll be *dangerous*. Half a star, though, and drop it like poison.

So, a review, of this system we've had for the last three years? Great!

Can I go first? It is freaking *hopeless*. Get rid of it. Call in Joe's Bulldozers and start again.

Why? Look, I could write a 10,000 word dissertation on how Big Food and Big Sugar have wrapped their tentacles and exerted their influence around what should be an entirely independent process, but do you need to know much more than the following?

Under the system, straight milk gets four stars, while Up and Go – with added, to use the specialised term – gunk – gets four and a half stars! Low-fat strawberry flavoured milk also gets four and a half stars! Some packets of chips even get four stars!

But packaged smoked salmon? Let's give that three and a half stars, while plain natural Greek yogurt falls away to one and a half stars. The Coles brand beer-battered frozen steakhouse chips get four stars. Milo, which is just under half sugar, gets four and a half stars. Nutri-Grain, which is about a third sugar, gets four stars. Commercial fruit juice, depending on the brand, gets between four and five stars. And yet the World Health Organization classifies fruit juice as containing "free" sugars that need to be restricted. So while as reputable an organisation as WHO says, "Don't drink it, Freddie", in Australia the government says it is about the healthiest thing you can drink. BS. Water is.

All up, notice a trend here?

While the science is in, and there is no doubt that the healthiest option is to choose simple, unprocessed food over processed food with endless crap added, the current Health Star system steers the masses from the edge of the supermarket where you can get the fresh products of Australian farmers to the long aisles where you get the products of Big Food and Big Sugar.

I repeat. Milo! Four and a half stars! Get it into your kids! And you know what, if I put strawberry flavoured milk on their Nutri-Grain and sprinkle it with Milo they will surely be BURSTING with good health.

How did the system get so corrupted?

Comprehending Practice Question 10

Explain the effects of language and structural choices in Text 10.

HANDY HINT
A writer's choice of language and structure can have numerous effects, such as emphasising a point; slowing the pace of reading; foreshadowing a plot development; creating contrast; contributing to a particular tone, voice or stylistic feature; and evoking interest, surprise or suspense.

10-minute activity

Read Text 10 and then complete the table below.

Language choice	Example from the text	Effect of language choice
Structural choice	**Example from the text**	**Effect of structural choice**

30-minute activity

Respond concisely to Comprehending Practice Question 10 in approximately 200–300 words.

60-minute activity

Compose a counterargument to Text 10 in the form of a persuasive response. Include at least one example of the following rhetorical devices:

- statistics
- rhetorical question
- anaphora
- expert opinion
- alliteration
- inclusive diction
- direct address
- hyperbole
- tricolon

Text 11

The following extract is taken from a fiction piece titled 'Spectrums' by Indigenous Australian author Allanah Hunt. It was published in *Griffith Review* 66, 2019.

THERE IS LIGHTNESS and darkness. Everyone knows that. There is a name for the shade that is neither light nor dark: grey. But there are multitudes of shades in between. No one has words for lightish grey or darkish light. Even the people who see more than black and white – the people who see the shades of grey – cannot comprehend the complexity of the colour spectrum. Remove one colour and a part of the world has been destroyed. You can add a little more light, maybe a dash of dark, but it will never replace the one colour that is no longer there.

It is missing.

LITHE AND FLUENT, Sandy runs like a pixie down the path between the ghost gums. Her hair streams out behind her bony shoulders like the piece of ribbon on a child's kite.

I would describe the colour of her hair to you, but colours have never meant much to me. I'm colourblind, you see. I have a rare congenital disease called rod monochromatism. This means all colours have been removed from my view, except the spectrums of black, white and grey. I'm unique. It can be taken as a compliment, really.

When I say I colourblind, people usually gasp in pity, saying, 'Oh, Elsie, how terrible, I never knew that!' or 'Bless you, Elsie, I would never want to wish that on anybody.' These reactions imply that I should be sad.

I suppose, at times, I've found it so – the thought that I'll never see what I've heard others call 'the vibrancy of velvet purple' or 'the brilliancy of bright yellow' makes me feel I'm missing out on something. On brighter days, my poor vision is diminished even more, and it's hard to make out any shape or person. The darker the day, the better my vision. It can be depressing.

But that's when a sliver of light catches through a window, casting a prism of lightness and darkness. Then, and only then, I know I couldn't possibly be missing out on something. How could I? Just look at that gorgeous shade of grey shimmering along my skin right now. Did anyone else notice that?

Comprehending Practice Question 11

Examine the impact of narrative point of view on developing voice in Text 11.

ACTIVITIES

10-minute activity

Read Text 11 and then complete the questions below in the spaces provided.

a What narrative point of view is used in the text?

____

b What are the effects of using this particular point of view?

____

____

____

c Use three adjectives to describe the tone of voice created in the text.

____

d What language or textual features have been used to create this tone?

____

____

30-minute activity

Respond concisely to Comprehending Practice Question 11 in approximately 200–300 words.

60-minute activity

Use Text 11 as the stimulus to create the opening to your own imaginative text. Follow these steps.

a Select a central character for your narrative who also views the world differently from others.

b Use the same narrative point of view as that used in Text 11.

c Highlight the following features in Text 11 and aim to use the same techniques in your own narrative: similes, dialogue, adverbs, alliteration, the imperative, disjunction, assonance.

d Follow the same structure and organisational sequence as that used in Text 11 to develop your narrative – note the length of sentences, syntax etc.

Text 12

The following black-and-white photograph was taken in a train station.

Comprehending Practice Question 12

How does Text 12 suggest multiple ideas about the modern world?

HANDY HINT

Although this question requires you to examine more than one idea suggested by the text, avoid simply listing all the examples you can think of. Select two or three ideas at most, so that you can explore them in detail.

10-minute activity

Carefully annotate Text 12, noting how ideas about the modern world are suggested by it. Concentrate on aspects of the text's construction, such as camera angle and shot type, proxemics and symbolism. Now brainstorm three ideas suggested by the text in the spaces provided below.

Idea 1: ____________________

Idea 2: ____________________

Idea 3: ____________________

30-minute activity

Respond concisely to Comprehending Practice Question 12 in approximately 200–300 words.

60-minute activity

a Familiarise yourself with the visual texts used in past ATAR examinations and their corresponding marking keys, available at https://senior-secondary.scsa.wa.edu.au/further-resources/past-atar-course-exams/english-past-atar-course-exams

b Design a marking guide appropriate for application to Comprehending Practice Question 12.

Text 13

The following is an abridged interview transcript from the ABC Radio program and podcast *Future Tense*, hosted by Antony Funnell on Radio National.

Antony Funnell: Now, as Jenine said, 'everyone uses mobile phones these days', and that statement provides the perfect segue into our final guest, Dr Katherine Moline from the Faculty of Art and Design at the University of New South Wales. Over the past year Katherine has run several workshops entitled Myths of the Near Future which has been all about exploring the relationship we have with those small rectangles of plastic and rare-earth metals that we obsessively carry around with us wherever we go.

Katherine Moline: It started from a series of works I'd done with phones and then mobile phones, just observing that people were ... their behaviours were changing. And I do a lot of teaching with media and communication design and have taught a lot of stuff around this in different exercises. So the workshop brought together those exercises, if you like, in a different series, which I've run with senior researchers down at RMIT and first-year design students at Griffith.

Antony Funnell: And these workshops are designed to get people rethinking the assumptions that they have about their relationship with smart phone technology.

Katherine Moline: Exactly. I mean, it comes from a very different angle than human computer interface researchers or people involved with classic ethnography. It's really looking at trying to shock or de-familiarise people's assumptions about their phones and how they use them.

Antony Funnell: So how do you go about doing that?

Katherine Moline: Well, I set a couple of pre-workshop activities, one is to read a JG Ballard short story called 'The Intensive Care Unit' from the 1970s, and another is to shadow or stalk a friend where they are using their mobile phone and to observe just the different interactions that happen. And the JG Ballard story is quite shocking, it really does predict webcams and talks about a family who meet the very first time after their entire family life being conducted via webcam. And it was written in the '70s. And how they unfortunately all murdered each other when they first met, they were so shocked at what they were really like when they weren't curated by TV.

Antony Funnell: So the idea is this curation aspect, isn't it, that many of us don't realise that while smart phones are terrific things, they are actually curating our lives in a way that other forms of technology haven't in the past.

Katherine Moline: Exactly. And [people have become] wisely or acutely self-conscious when they are using their phones, so they have become branding mechanisms, not often heartfelt, raw gossip that you might have heard on the telephone previously. But particularly when people use images they are curating their own lives. So that really changes things.

Antony Funnell: So we think about communication devices as just that, as communication devices. We often don't realise, do we, that they are also part of storytelling, the storytelling of our own lives.

Comprehending Practice Question 13

Analyse how Text 13 encourages the audience to reflect on their own viewpoints.

10-minute activity

In your own words, summarise two assumptions explored in the text.

Assumption 1: ______________________________

____

Assumption 2: ______________________________

____

30-minute activity

Respond concisely to Comprehending Practice Question 13 in approximately 200–300 words.

60-minute activity

a Complete the 30-minute activity above.

b Apply the following checklist to your response.

	YES	NO
Did you annotate the text according to the focus of the question?		
Did you briefly plan your response?		
Did you understand all the words of the question?		
Did you properly read the contextual information provided and use it to your advantage?		
Have you engaged with the question meaningfully from your opening sentence (the thesis)?		
Have you divided your response logically into paragraphs (if necessary)?		
Have you included several short quotes to support your points?		
Have you avoided using overly lengthy quotes (full, long sentences)?		
Are the quotes smoothly embedded into your own sentences?		
Have you used the quotes as support rather than letting them make the points for you?		
Have you written between 200 and 300 words?		
Is your writing clear and expressive, using correct punctuation, spelling and grammar?		

c Type your response, editing and improving it where necessary.

Text 14

The following image is a greyscale version of a still from the SBS television miniseries *The Hunting* (2019). It shows the moment when the central character discovers her private image is being shared online.

Comprehending Practice Question 14

Discuss the role of the audience in making meaning of this text.

HANDY HINT Consider how an audience's personal context and prior experience may contribute to the inferences they make about the text's meaning.

10-minute activity

Compile a list of points in the following table in response to Text 14.

Composition	Written text	Visual images	Conventions
Consider layout arrangement, foregrounding etc.	Consider register, connotations, typography etc.	Consider shot types, angles, symbolism, gaze etc.	Consider conventions of television series, social media websites etc.

30-minute activity

Respond concisely to Comprehending Practice Question 14 in approximately 200–300 words.

60-minute activity

a Using the advice offered on page 7 of this book, design 10 new Section One questions that reflect a wide sampling of the syllabus examinable content and that could be suitably applied to Text 14.

b Produce a brief plan for a response to five of the new questions you have designed.

Text 15

The following text is titled 'An Open Letter to the Phrase "Positive Vibes Only"'. It was published on the American website *McSweeney's Internet Tendency* in 2018. The site showcases short works of humour submitted by both aspiring and established writers.

Dear "Positive Vibes Only,"

Look at you, you're everywhere. You're really having a minute. Inscribed on the moisture-wicking tank tops of upper-class yoga practitioners; cropping up in the captions of Instagram wellness models; peppered into the mission statements of for-profit organizations. You're like the I VOTED sticker for people with privilege and unwavering levels of serotonin, and here's why I'm going to need you to die:

There are many things that the power of positive thought can't band-aid let alone fix right now. Things like pervasive social structural injustice, economic disparity, stagnant job markets, the prohibitive cost of healthcare, sexism, Nazism, global warming, shuttering libraries, disappearing bees, diminished attention spans, endemic loneliness, the opioid crisis, the misogyny of the president, recklessly armed citizens, the Kardashians, Oreo Thins, pre-teens eating Tide Pods etc.

And YOU, a cognitive bias posturing as a catchphrase that's screen-printed on every viable surface, aren't doing jack to solve any of it. You're a passive little phrase engineered to move merch and you're missing the dang point.

At best, "Positive Vibes Only" sounds like a poorly branded free clinic. At worst, it makes disengaging from reality in favor of wishful thinking a lifestyle aspiration, which in 2018 is just mother-effing dangerous. The semantics of "PVO" doesn't just pollute more tinder bios than I can swipe a thumb at, but far worse it rejects diversity of opinion and experience from the Rightfully Sad. Depressed Folk. Marginalized Folk. Trying Folk. Folk who are navigating tremendous amounts of suffering and trauma by grieving, raging, organizing and healing — and who require space and conversations to do so.

What you do, "Positive Vibes Only," is shame and exclude people who cannot happy-think their way out of their realities. People who can't hashtag their way out of systemic oppression, sexual assault, defaulting mortgages, familial displacement, serious mood disorders, terminal illness and the like.

What the world needs now is not positive thinking — what the world needs now is disruptive, revolutionary thinking. And action. And that requires getting sad, mad and organized.

So peace out, "Positive Vibes Only." It ain't all good and those of us seeking justice are not going to pretend otherwise.

You're not welcome.

— Ali O'Reilly

Comprehending Practice Question 15

Show how textual features are used in Text 15 to construct a distinctive voice.

10-minute activity

a Use three different coloured highlighters to identify the following features used throughout Text 15:

- verbs
- direct address
- listing

b Think of three adjectives to describe the voice constructed in Text 15 and write them in the spaces below.

__________________ __________________ __________________

30-minute activity

Respond concisely to Comprehending Practice Question 15 in approximately 200–300 words.

60-minute activity

a Brainstorm a list of popular modern expressions, idioms and/or acronyms in the space below.
e.g. YOLO (You Only Live Once)

____

____

____

____

____

____

b Now attempt to use the same distinctive tone of voice as that constructed in Text 15 to create your own open letter addressed to one of the above.

Text 16

The following text is an edited extract from a contemporary novel by Neil Grant titled *The Honeyman and the Hunter*. It is a coming-of-age story about Rudra, an Indian-Australian boy, who lives in a fishing town in Australia.

RUDRA SOLACE IS CROSSING THE CHANNEL with his best mate, Maggs Briley – Rudra with his heart clambering in his chest and Maggs powering through, born to it. The summer storm has left bruises in the sky – great welts of cloud up high and others, blotchy stains, above the headland. Last night's rain set the creeks to flooding, vomiting branches and beer cans from the neck of Brisbane Water. The outward tide is in their favour, helping them to the break that is spitting and cracking in the middle distance.

This is a sharky paddle – all the talk that ever was points to it. 'Men in grey suits' hazing boats. A local nabbed by a tiger off Lobster Beach last summer (or the one before), returning shaken and pulpy, stitched and glued back together at Gosford Hospital.

We are just meat, thinks Rudra. Him on his old six-four with glass as yellow as a smoker's fingers. This board has lived for too long beneath his house, that much is obvious. *She'll never win a beauty contest*, as Maggs says, *but at least she floats*. Rudra isn't a surfer, not really, but when your best mate calls and school's out for summer, you have to go. Maggs, on the other hand, has a brand-new McCoy he's been saving for this swell. He snaps at least one board a season – pulling in when he should not, in Rudra's opinion. Maggs has neoprene skin. He fits well here on the Central Coast.

The paddle is long and brutal, and Rudra's arms are burning by the time they reach the line-up. There are a couple of guys from school here and some older surfers on longboards. Rudra doesn't know the school guys well – ex year twelves, finished exams and back at year zero. They were once the gods of the corridors and open spaces, cruel rulers. Now they are fallen.

One of them is called Judge Dredd; sometimes just Judge. Because of his dreads, Rudra imagines, or maybe because everyone just dreads being around him. Not much going on upstairs with these guys – they will never conquer the world.

The first wave of the set breaks – tumbling wide, sucking Maggs up and spitting him down the face.

Rudra sits there for a moment, stilling his heart. The next one in the set is smaller and one of the long boarders paddles hard, moving his whole upper body like a beached seal, legs beating the air behind him. But he misses, slapping the water in disgust as it carries on towards the year zeros, and to Rudra.

Rudra is in the perfect position. The wave knows it too – willing him on, throwing out little fringes of white from its lip. And the sun sneaks through, and it's all going to be okay. He sets up for the barrel – one of only three in his whole surfing life so far. Judge is already shrouded in foam, sucking gulps of sand. Maggs, paddling back out, rips a howl that blesses this wave and their friendship and makes this a sacred run at whatever. And the wave stretches on and on and folds over like a blanket and Rudra crouches and drives for the winking eye of headland and then he is out into the summer air and the sea is hissing like Dr Pepper.

Comprehending Practice Question 16

Explain how attitudes are revealed through aspects of characterisation in Text 16.

HANDY HINT Note that 'attitudes' is plural in this question, which means you need to identify more than one. An attitude can be defined as a general outlook, viewpoint or feeling towards or about something.

ACTIVITIES

10-minute activity

Read and annotate Text 16, then complete the table below.

Identify three attitudes revealed through a character.	How are these attitudes revealed through aspects of characterisation (e.g. actions, thoughts, interactions, dialogue)?
1	
2	
3	

30-minute activity

Respond concisely to Comprehending Practice Question 16 in approximately 200–300 words.

60-minute activity

a Complete the 30-minute activity above.

b Select a one-page extract from an imaginative text you are studying or have studied this year. Apply Comprehending Question 16 to it and respond concisely in approximately 200–300 words.

c Now create an analytical comparison between Text 16 and your studied text extract by responding to the following question in approximately 200–300 words.

Compare how the texts have revealed the attitudes of a character.

Text 17A

This text is a film poster for the 1994 Australian film *The Adventures of Priscilla, Queen of the Desert*, which is about three drag queens who venture to the Australian outback to perform.

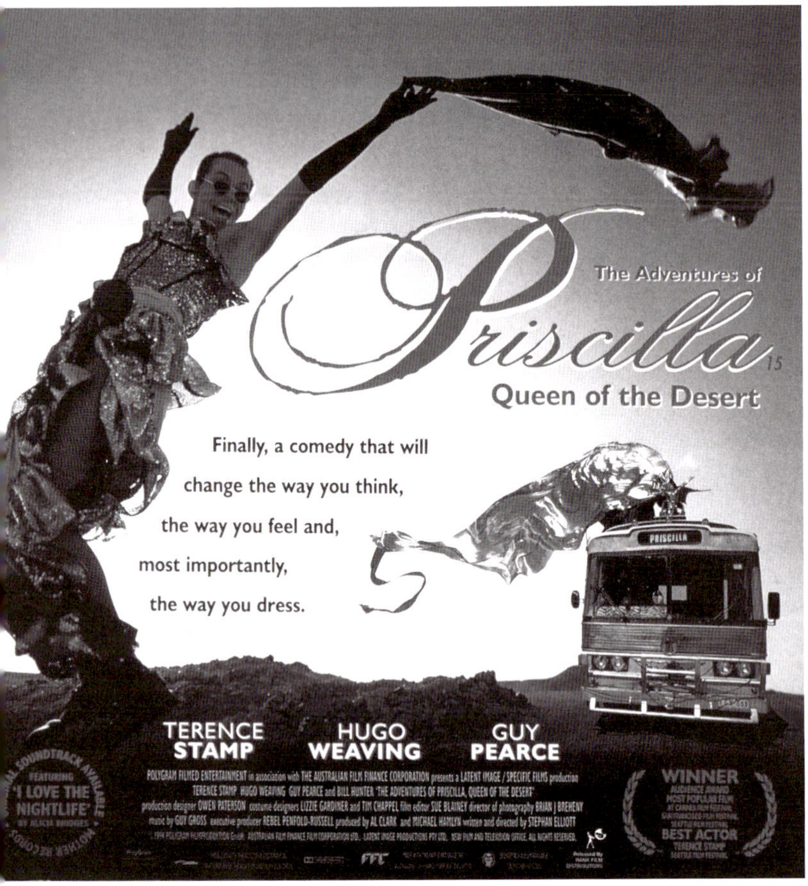

Text 17B

This text is a movie poster for the film *On the Basis of Sex* (2018), which depicts the life of Ruth Bader Ginsburg, a lawyer and gender equality advocate in the 1970s, and the second woman to be appointed an Associate Justice of the Supreme Court in the United States.

Comprehending Practice Question 17

Compare the features used in Texts A and B to represent people involved in cultural change.

10-minute activity

Identify the cultural change you think is evident in each text. Consider aspects of a dominant culture or ideology that the people in each image might be challenging, and how this challenge is evident in the texts' visual and written language features. Take into account the context of production of each text, as specified in the text descriptors.

Text A: Cultural change	Text B: Cultural change
Text A: Visual and written techniques	**Text B: Visual and written techniques**

30-minute activity

Respond concisely to Comprehending Practice Question 17 in approximately 200–300 words.

60-minute activity

a Find a multimodal text (film poster, graphic novel extract, advertisement etc.) that highlights a similar representation of people involved in cultural change.

b Annotate and analyse the text according to its use of visual and written language features and how they shape this representation of people.

c Brainstorm a list of contextual factors (considering social, political, cultural and historical contexts) that might shape this representation of people in the text.

d Write a response, in 200–300 words, to Comprehending Practice Question 17, with reference to the text you chose.

Text 18

The following text is an extract from a piece of travel writing by Andrew Bain, titled 'Cruising the Kimberley and Horizontal Falls: Australia's most unusual natural wonder'. It was originally published on the *Traveller* website by *The Sydney Morning Herald* and *The Age*.

On the Kimberley coastline, the tide is turning. High tide has been, and now it's as though somebody has pulled the plug on the ocean. Millions of litres of ocean sucks through a narrow sea gorge, the water brawling and churning as it goes. And we're about to head through it in a boat.

I've come on Silversea's Silver Discoverer ship, which has anchored in Talbot Bay on our first full day out from Broome. Seemingly enclosed by hills, the bay looks and feels like a lagoon, with water that's almost the blue of a glacial lake.

In the fast boat, we skim across the bay to the mouth of the Horizontal Waterfalls, where tides as high as 13 metres squish through two gorges with rust-red walls that are as close as seven metres apart.

During the highest tides, as much as one million litres of water pours through the gaps every second. We've had the fortune (good or bad, depending on your perspective) to arrive on a neap tide of just four to five metres. The next few minutes are going to be like a dress rehearsal of the full natural fury that can occur here.

"This is the most dangerous current in the Kimberley," the skipper, Adrian, announces. And with that, we're going in, bouncing across the water like a vehicle on a corrugated desert track. In the middle of the gap, Adrian slows the boat and then suddenly we're idling, as though we're gently parking in the middle of a storm.

"The water's running at 12km/h here," he reads from the boat's gadgetry, but this is the widest and most placid of the two gaps. By the time we're idling again inside the narrower gorge, less than a kilometre ahead, the water's flooding through at 23km/h. When we turn and head back through the gorge, travelling with the flow, it's like being sucked through a straw, the water surging so fast it's literally flowing downhill, creating a step of water at the end of the gorge. Today the step is just half a metre in height, which is daunting enough when you're about to plunge over it, but when it gets above one or two metres, boats can't get through, the angle of the step stranding their motors out of the water.

Incredibly, there's a force around Talbot Bay even more powerful than the Horizontal Waterfalls. In the afternoon, we board the Silver Discoverer's zodiacs and head to the bay's end, funnelling into Cyclone Creek.

As the eyes of a crocodile roll past like marbles, we head upstream and into the sort of prehistory that's beyond comprehension. The Kimberley was once separated from the rest of Australia, and Cyclone Creek is pretty much along the line where the two landmasses are thought to have collided. Above the river, the towering orange cliffs bristle with spinifex, and there are ramparts of rock that look like defensive walls constructed by humans – the Great Wall of Australia.

As we edge in closer to the cliffs, their most striking feature becomes apparent. These rocks said to be 1.7 billion years old – almost half the age of the Earth – are bent, buckled and scrunched up like paper, testifying to the cataclysmic force that shaped them when the lands came together. Against this, even the Horizontal Waterfalls seem like a gentle brook.

Comprehending Practice Question 18

How do the language features in the text establish a sense of danger?

HANDY HINT

Note that the question does not include a specific command word such as 'analyse' or 'explain'. The type of response is implied by 'how', guiding you to concentrate on the workings and function of the language features; analysis will be embedded naturally within an effective response.

ACTIVITIES

10-minute activity

a Brainstorm a list of language features used in Text 18 in the space below.

____

____

____

____

b Now annotate the text, noting the purpose and effect of these features.

30-minute activity

Respond concisely to Comprehending Practice Question 18 in approximately 200–300 words.

60-minute activity

a Although Text 18 is nonfiction, it is still telling a 'story' with an identifiable narrative plot structure. Re-create the diagram below and plot the development of action or events, from beginning to end, that create a sense of danger in this extract. Include observations about how the author uses language features in order to create this sense of danger.

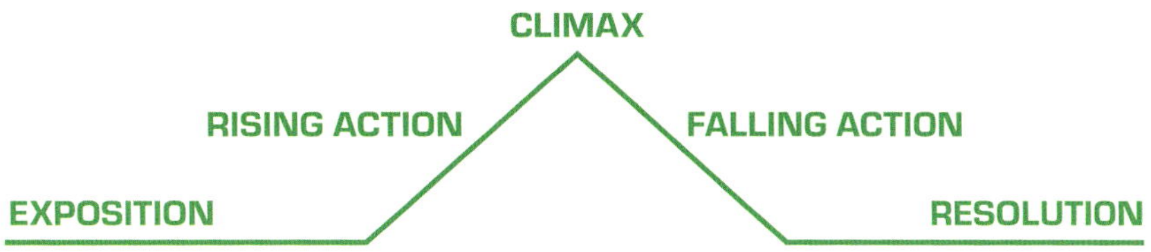

b Select an exciting, dangerous or fear-inducing experience from your life and use the diagram above to plan a response that tells the story of this event.

c Write a list of language features that you could use to engage your reader.

d Compose the text in full.

Text 19

The following text is a reproduction of the front page of *The West Australian* newspaper on 4 January 2020.

Picture: Danella Bevis

EXCLUSIVE New recruits wanted as thinning ranks of volunteer fireys battle the summer from hell

HEROES WELCOME

JOANNA DELALANDE

West Australians are being encouraged to become volunteer firefighters amid a slump in numbers.

SPECIAL REPORT P9

SPIRIT OF DUNKIRK IN FIRE EXODUS PAGES 6-7

Comprehending Practice Question 19

With reference to visual construction, account for two different interpretations of Text 19.

HANDY HINT An interpretation is your understanding of a text's meaning and its effects. There can be multiple interpretations of texts because responses to them are shaped by a variety of contextual factors.

ACTIVITIES

10-minute activity

Annotate Text 19 using the following questions as a guide.

- a What is the focal point of this image?
- b Identify a call to action in the image. Which visual and/or written language features construct this call to action? Who does it target? Why?
- c What is the effect of the historical allusion to 'Dunkirk' in the pointer at the bottom of the page?
- d What observations can you make about the body language, stance, facial expressions, gaze and proximity of the subjects?
- e What observations can you make about the subjects' age, gender, ethnicity etc.?
- f What is an audience's role in making meaning from the text? What factors might influence their interpretation of this image?
- g What is your interpretation of this image? Why?
- h What could be an alternative interpretation? Why?

30-minute activity

Respond concisely to Comprehending Practice Question 19 in approximately 200–300 words.

60-minute activity

- a Locate the definitions for the terms 'reading' and 'readings' in your course glossary. Ensure that you understand the terms 'dominant', 'alternative' and 'resistant' readings.
- b Now develop an alternative or resistant reading of one of your studied texts by applying the following Responding-style question to it. Write an analytical essay in response to the question.

Explain the factors that have led you to develop an alternative or resistant reading of a studied text.

Text 20

The following is an edited extract from a speech by then Australian Prime Minister Julia Gillard. It was delivered at a 2013 International Women's Day breakfast.

I acknowledge each of you – the women drawn here by the power of this day. You are women of achievement. Women who reach out to shape the future. This is a day of celebration, and rightly so. Even if the women's movement had changed just one life, it would be worth it. Yet over the past century, it has changed millions of lives, including my own.

But today our celebration must be tempered by realism. The first International Women's Day was 102 years ago. This is an old struggle. Yet the level of assault and abuse is still too high. The gender pay gap is still too wide. The number of women in senior roles is still too few. We should be impatient. It's time to get a move on. And friends, let's never forget that women's rights are indivisible. If women are marginalised or oppressed anywhere, it's as though it happened to one of us. This year America has been celebrating 150 years since President Lincoln ended slavery. We imagine slavery as something from the pages of history. But it's not.

It's hard to imagine from the safety and comfort we know, yet slavery still exists in our world and in our land. The setting is different than it once was. Today the people forced into slavery work in factories, in domestic servitude, in brothels. But the violence and coercion they face is the same. In February this year I had the opportunity to meet with two victims of human trafficking. They had been brought to Australia by their employers under false pretences. They had their passports taken. They weren't allowed to leave the house without supervision. One of them wasn't paid properly; the other wasn't paid at all. When they challenged their employers, they were abused and threatened.

That occurred here, in Australia. Not 150 years ago but in the last three years ...

Since 2004, Australia has invested over $150 million in anti-people-trafficking measures, in our region and here at home.

But as Australia's first female Prime Minister, I've wanted us to do even more. That's why we passed the Slavery, Slavery-like Conditions and People Trafficking Act which our Governor-General signed into law yesterday. This Act creates new offences of forced marriage and harbouring a victim. It enables accomplices to be charged as well as the main perpetrators. It raises the penalties for existing debt bondage offences, and also increases payments to victims ...

Friends, this is one of the many ways that Australia is saying 'no'.

No to people trafficking.

No to slavery.

No to treating women like objects or chattels.

That is not a world we will accept.

That is not a life we want for any woman or any girl.

Not here.

Not overseas.

Not anywhere.

Not ever.

And so, on International Women's Day, we affirm this simple but enduring truth: change is always possible, and the hope we share can never be in vain.

Comprehending Practice Question 20

Evaluate whether this text fulfils a persuasive purpose through the perspective it offers.

HANDY HINT The command word 'evaluate' means to make a critical judgement or to appraise carefully. Consider the extent to which the text is successful in convincing you or the wider audience to adopt the viewpoint promoted.

ACTIVITIES

10-minute activity

Read and annotate Text 20 and then respond to the questions below in dot-point form.

a What topic, issue or idea does the perspective relate to?

b Who does the perspective belong to? Does the owner represent a larger group or ideology?

c What is the viewpoint associated with the perspective?

d What contextual factors have likely shaped or influenced this viewpoint?

e How do you know this is the viewpoint? What textual features have been used to communicate it? Consider features such as direct address, tone and rhetorical devices.

f To what extent are these features persuasive?

30-minute activity

Respond concisely to Comprehending Practice Question 20 in approximately 200–300 words.

60-minute activity

a Watch former Australian Prime Minister Julia Gillard's famous 'Misogyny Speech', accessible at: https://www.youtube.com/watch?v=fCNuPcf8L00.

b As you view and listen to the speech, note down some of the similarities between the ideas she expresses there and in Text 20.

c Now compose your own persuasive speech, using some of the language, structural and stylistic techniques used in both texts. Select your own topic to write about, but use Text 20 as a model to sequence your response. Note its effective use of syntax and repetition.

CHAPTER 3

Responding Practice

This chapter addresses the demands of Section Two of the examination. It includes 15 different practice questions that require an understanding of a wide sampling of the examinable content from the syllabus in relation to studied texts. A working time of 60 minutes is recommended for each of these questions. This reflects the demands of Section Two of the exam, in which you need to answer one question out of a possible six within this suggested time frame. This chapter also includes the following features.

- A 10-minute activity accompanying each practice question provides scaffolded support to help decode the question effectively and to plan a response.
- A 20-minute activity accompanying each practice question generally provides an opportunity to consider the question more closely, to produce a detailed plan, to identify suitable evidence from your studied texts, and to write and/or reflect on part of a response, such as an introduction or body paragraph.
- Brief 'handy hints' accompany some of the questions which may present particular pitfalls; the hints direct you away from potential misreadings of the questions.

WHAT TO EXPECT IN SECTION TWO

This is what you can expect to encounter in the Responding section.

- The questions will be aligned closely to the syllabus. Of course, they can never reflect all of the examinable content, due to the limitations of only six questions being available. This is why it is crucial that you have a good grasp of the syllabus in its entirety and are prepared to be assessed on any part of it.

- You will likely need to consider the relationship between at least two or three different syllabus concepts. The questions in this section can be complex and multilayered. Rather than investing all your energy into preparing for 'a perspective question' or 'a context question', it is more beneficial to understand how the complete bullet points from the syllabus – which contextualise these key syllabus concepts – can be applied to your studied texts.
- You will probably have to write a response to a question that is unlike any you have encountered previously in class assessments or semester exams. The chances of you encountering exactly the same questions again are virtually nil. The more adaptable your textual examples are, the easier it will be to transfer your knowledge and understandings of your studied text/s to a new question.
- You will only be able to confidently decide which studied text/s to refer to once you see the questions in the examination. Revise several studied texts so that you have the option to answer any of the questions. The best text to use is *always* going to be the one most suited to answering the question you select on the day. You may refer to any studied text – there is no hierarchy in terms of preferred text length, mode or medium.
- Try to use personal voice if the question includes an invitation to do so through its use of words such as 'you' or 'your'. Using personal pronouns such as 'I' or 'me' in your response is not only acceptable for a question of this nature, it is actually encouraged.

TYPES OF QUESTIONS IN SECTION TWO

The requirement in this section is that you apply the selected question to a text or texts that you have studied. The questions usually feature a directive in the form of a command word, together with syllabus concept words and phrases derived from the examinable content. The questions are also likely to include condition and critical words that provide more specific guidance and nuance. The terms 'command', 'concept', 'condition' and 'critical' are explained on page 2. The questions in this section lend themselves to the writing of a complete analytical essay.

Sample Section Two question: Responding

Compare the ways in which **two** texts explore similar ideas or issues despite being created in different contexts.

The most important considerations for the types of questions in this section are:

- understanding the nuances of different command words
- being able to identify the specific syllabus concepts and examinable content being assessed
- responding to critical words that work to differentiate between the quality of responses.

Questions in this section are often broader and more open than those in Section One. For instance, they may include more generalised terms such as 'an idea', rather than specifying what that idea relates to (as is sometimes the case in the Comprehending section). This is because the questions in Section Two need to be accessible to a large number of candidates from different schools throughout the state, who study a diverse range of texts containing widely varying ideas.

The types of questions included in this section often require you to:

- interrogate the assumptions, perspectives, attitudes and values that underpin your studied text or texts
- compare and/or contrast two studied texts by identifying their similarities and differences
- consider the relationship between syllabus concepts
- reflect on your own context, responses, interpretations, attitudes and values in relation to your studied text/s
- recall quotes and appropriate evidence from your studied text/s in order to support your argument.

This section provides an excellent opportunity for you to showcase a deep understanding of the syllabus content in relation to your studied text/s. However, it is worth noting that any one question will simply not provide the scope for you to detail *everything* you know about the text/s. Although this may feel disappointing to you, rest assured that it is always better to answer the selected question in a tightly focused and discerning manner than to include irrelevant details in an excessively long response.

TOP TIPS FOR SECTION TWO

There are many ways to revise your texts and prepare thoroughly for Section Two of the examination, as outlined on pages 8–9. The following tips summarise the important advice for achieving success in this section during the examination itself.

- Choose your question carefully. Read all six, thinking about your understanding of their syllabus concepts and the potential application of your knowledge to answering them. Note that all questions are considered equal in terms of difficulty – *all* questions have a possible 40 marks available. If you perceive that a particular question is 'easy' relative to the others, that just means you have prepared well for it – it is probably in your best interests to pick that one!
- Deconstruct the selected question carefully. Identify its command, concept, condition and critical words. Some candidates find it helpful to think of synonyms for some of the words in the question.
- Plan! This process is critical in terms of focusing your thoughts and providing you with a clear framework. A plan only needs to be brief, with a few dot points.
- Start with a clear introduction that provides a brief overview of the text/s to be examined. Write a clear, well-constructed thesis statement that engages fully with all aspects of the question.
- Ensure that body paragraphs include a clear topic sentence that connects back to the question. Points should be supported with plenty of specific and carefully selected textual evidence.
- When you start and finish each paragraph, remind yourself of the question to ensure that you are not deviating from it. Use transition markers to enhance cohesion and overall structure.
- Round out your essay with a powerful end which extends beyond the question to comment on the text's broader meaning/s, teachings or implications.
- Adhere to the recommended working time of 60 minutes. While the extra weighting of this section allows you to benefit from the study of your texts, it does not indicate that more time should be spent on it. A lengthy response *is not* necessarily a good one; the quality of your response can be compomised if you write too much.

PRACTICE QUESTIONS AND ACTIVITIES

This section contains a variety of practice questions and activities to develop your skills.

Responding Practice Question 1

Analyse how the language, structural and stylistic choices evident within one text have influenced your response to it.

HANDY HINT The use of the word 'your' in the question signals that you are required to use personal voice. Make sure your response incorporates personal pronouns such as 'I' and 'me' to engage with this component of the question.

ACTIVITIES

10-minute activity

In the table below, make a list of language, structural and stylistic features used in one of your studied texts.

Language features	Structural features	Stylistic features

20-minute activity

a Complete the 10-minute activity above.

b Now compare your points with those listed in the Sample Marking Guide provided on pages 95–6. Using the information in the marking guide, make any alterations and additions required to the table above.

60-minute activity

With reference to one of your studied texts, write a full analytical response to Responding Practice Question 1. Your response should demonstrate your critical thinking skills.

Responding Practice Question 2

Discuss how one text's central themes relate to multiple contextual factors relevant at the time of its creation.

ACTIVITIES

10-minute activity

Read Responding Practice Question 2 above and, in the spaces below, identify its:

command word/s: ______________________________

concept word/s: ______________________________

condition word/s: ______________________________

critical word/s: ______________________________

(Refer to page 2 for an explanation of these terms.)

20-minute activity

a With reference to one of your studied texts, plan a response to Responding Practice Question 2 in the table below by briefly listing the main point/s of each paragraph.

	Paragraph 1	Paragraph 2	Paragraph 3
Central theme			
Contextual factors			

b Now use your plan to produce an introduction for a response to the question.

60-minute activity

With reference to one of your studied texts, write a full analytical response to Responding Practice Question 2. Your response should demonstrate your critical thinking skills.

Responding Practice Question 3

With reference to at least one text, explore the function of voice in highlighting a specific attitude.

HANDY HINT Keep in mind that attitudes are always generated **towards** something or **about** something. Make sure your response clearly identifies what this 'something' is (e.g. an issue, a topic, a character, a setting).

ACTIVITIES

10-minute activity

Highlight the key words in Responding Practice Question 3 and, around the question, jot down your planning notes.

20-minute activity

Drawing on the plan you created in the previous activity, write an introduction for your response in the space below. After you have written the introduction, take at least five minutes to edit your work, checking it for clarity, expression and grammar, punctuation and spelling errors.

60-minute activity

With reference to at least one of your studied texts, write a full analytical response to Responding Practice Question 3. Your response should demonstrate your critical thinking skills.

Responding Practice Question 4

Discuss why the audience response to a text may vary between different cultural contexts.

10-minute activity

Identify the key words in Responding Practice Question 4 and find synonyms for them. Now rewrite the question in your own words in the space below.

20-minute activity

With reference to a studied text, complete the following table to plan a response to Responding Practice Question 4.

Cultural contexts			
Audience response/s			
Reasons for audience response/s			

60-minute activity

With reference to one of your studied texts, write a full analytical response to Responding Practice Question 4. Your response should demonstrate your critical thinking skills.

Responding Practice Question 5

Compare the treatment of a similar idea explored within two texts of different modes or genres.

ACTIVITIES

10-minute activity

With reference to two studied texts, complete the following Venn diagram to plan a response to Responding Practice Question 5.

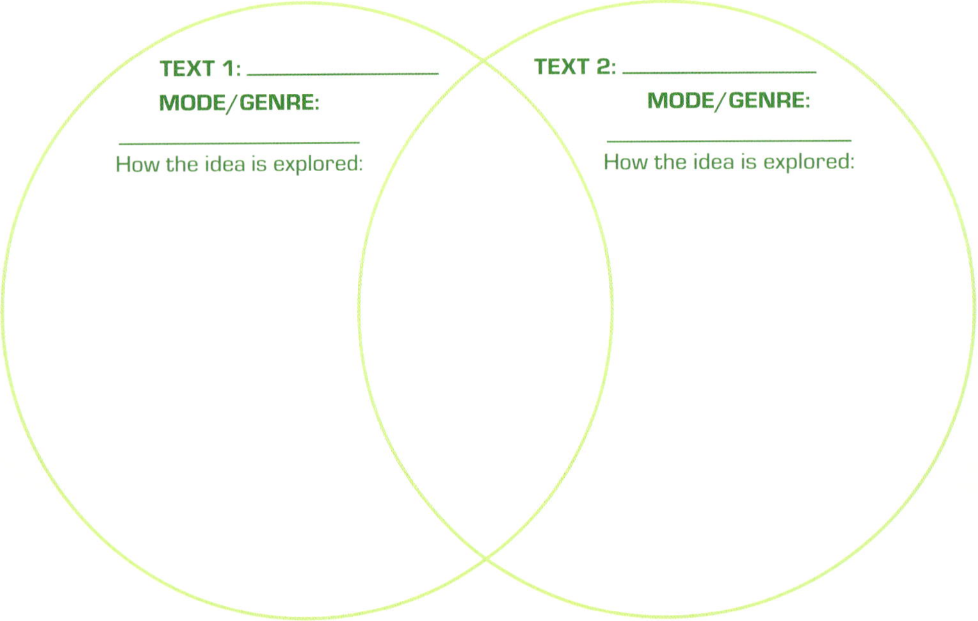

20-minute activity

a Spend 15 minutes drafting a comparative body paragraph that responds to Responding Practice Question 5.

b Use an additional five minutes to highlight its 'compare' and 'contrast' terminology (e.g. both, similarly, in contrast to, on the other hand, likewise, whereas).

60-minute activity

With reference to two of your studied texts, write a full analytical response to Responding Practice Question 5. Your response should demonstrate your critical thinking skills.

Responding Practice Question 6

With reference to one text, evaluate the role that language features have played in generating controversy or empathy.

HANDY HINT Don't forget that 'language features' are evident in visual, spoken and multimodal texts as well as in written texts. A film may use visual language techniques such as framing, proxemics and composition, as well as auditory language such as character dialogue and background music.

ACTIVITIES

10-minute activity

With reference to a studied text, complete the following graphic organiser to plan a response to Responding Practice Question 6.

TEXT:

Language feature 1:

Language feature 2:

Language feature 3:

Summarise the role of these features in generating controversy *or* empathy (not both!) by producing a thesis statement.

Consider *why* they have generated such responses. Have the features played a significant role or a minor one?

THESIS STATEMENT:

20-minute activity

Compile a list of textual evidence and quotes from a studied text that could be used to support your answer to Responding Practice Question 6.

60-minute activity

With reference to one of your studied texts, write a full analytical response to Responding Practice Question 6. Your response should demonstrate your critical thinking skills.

Responding Practice Question 7

Analyse the extent to which a text meets the expectations of its genre in order to shape an audience response.

ACTIVITIES

10-minute activity

Locate the examinable content that Practice Responding Question 7 corresponds to in the ATAR syllabus. Write the syllabus point/s in full below.

____

____

____

20-minute activity

With reference to one of your studied texts and Responding Practice Question 7, complete the following table.

Text title:			
Genre of text:			
Expectations of the genre (consider its accepted conventions, your prior experience with the genre etc.)		Met or not met?	Effect/s of expectation being met or not met on audience response
Expectation 1			
Expectation 2			
Expectation 3			

60-minute activity

With reference to one of your studied texts, write a full analytical response to Responding Practice Question 7. Your response should demonstrate your critical thinking skills.

Responding Practice Question 8

Discuss how the dominant perspective represented in one text is used to promote particular values.

10-minute activity

Locate the syllabus examinable content that Responding Practice Question 8 corresponds to. Devise two new Responding-style questions using the same stem phrase.

1 ____

____

____

2 ____

____

____

20-minute activity

Select a studied text that emphasises or privileges one perspective over others, such as the perspective of a protagonist in a narrative or the orator of a speech. Apply the following questions to the text, recording your answers in sentence form.

- **a** Who does this main perspective belong to? Can this owner be read as representative of a larger social or cultural group?
- **b** What is the viewpoint associated with the perspective?
- **c** What contextual influences have contributed to this perspective?
- **d** What specific values underpin the viewpoints represented in the text?
- **e** What textual features are used to represent the perspective and its associated values?

60-minute activity

With reference to one of your studied texts, write a full analytical response to Responding Practice Question 8. Your response should demonstrate your critical thinking skills.

Responding Practice Question 9

Through a comparison of two texts, explain how the distinctive features of a specific genre have evolved over time.

HANDY HINT

Select two texts belonging to the same genre (such as science fiction or dystopian fiction; or, if you prefer to use a genre of form and structure, short stories or feature articles). They should reflect different production contexts; that is, the texts were created or produced during different periods of time.

ACTIVITIES

10-minute activity

Re-create the table below and complete it with reference to three different genres you have studied over the course of Years 11 and 12.

Genre			
List of distinctive features			

20-minute activity

Select a specific genre you have studied. Now add approximate dates or time periods above the time line, as well as a list of distinctive features and conventions corresponding to these time frames below the time line, to indicate how the genre has evolved and changed over time.

GENRE: ____________________

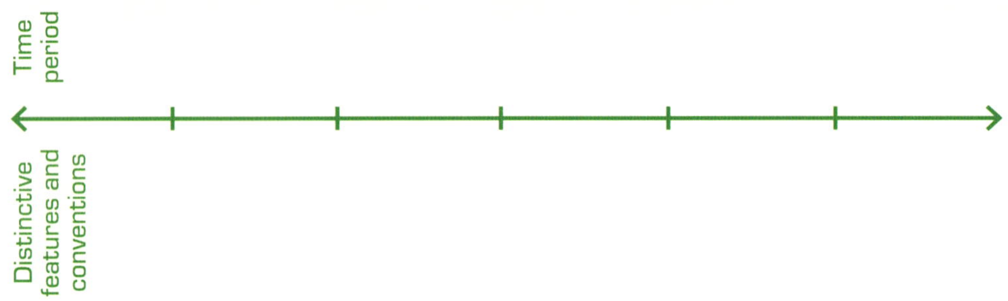

60-minute activity

With reference to two of your studied texts, write a full analytical response to Responding Practice Question 9. Your response should demonstrate your critical thinking skills.

Responding Practice Question 10

Discuss how your response to a text has been influenced by its voice and narrative point of view.

HANDY HINT This question lends itself to a discussion of one of your studied imaginative narrative texts, such as a novel or short story.

10-minute activity

In the table below, list three different types of narrative point of view and an example of a text that uses each type of point of view.

Type of narrative point of view	Text example

20-minute activity

In the space below, compile a list of textual evidence and quotes from a studied text that could be used to support your answer to Responding Practice Question 10.

60-minute activity

With reference to one of your studied texts, write a full analytical response to Responding Practice Question 10. Your response should demonstrate your critical thinking skills.

Responding Practice Question 11

How has the transformation or adaptation of a text into a different medium changed its meaning?

HANDY HINT

While this question does not include the command word 'compare', it does lend itself to a comparison of two texts, in which one is the transformation or adaptation of the other into a different medium. Examples include the novel *Wake in Fright*, which has been transformed or adapted into both a film and a television series, and the novel *The Handmaid's Tale*, which has been adapted into a television series.

ACTIVITIES

10-minute activity

Refer to the course glossary or a dictionary to locate definitions for the following key terms.

medium: ____________________

transformation: ____________________

adaptation: ____________________

meaning: ____________________

20-minute activity

Complete the table with reference to two studied texts, one of which has been transformed or adapted into a different medium to create the other.

	Original medium	New medium	Change in meaning
Structural features			
Language features			
Stylistic features			

60-minute activity

With reference to two of your studied texts, write a full analytical response to Responding Practice Question 11. Your response should demonstrate your critical thinking skills.

Responding Practice Question 12

Reflect upon how and why different perspectives are represented within one studied text.

10-minute activity

In Responding Practice Question 12, the command word 'reflect' means to think carefully or consider deeply. In the space below, list words or phrases that you might use in your writing to articulate your reflections on a studied text.

e.g. *Upon reflection, I found myself thinking ...*

- ______________________
- ______________________
- ______________________
- ______________________
- ______________________
- ______________________

20-minute activity

Re-create the table below and complete it with reference to one studied text. You may decide to add another row for a third perspective.

	Summarise the perspective (viewpoint + context)	*How* is the perspective represented through features of the text?	*Why* is this perspective represented in the text? What purpose does it serve?
Perspective 1			
Perspective 2			

60-minute activity

With reference to one of your studied texts, write a full analytical response to Responding Practice Question 12. Your response should demonstrate your critical thinking skills.

Responding Practice Question 13

Discuss why you have developed a more considered interpretation of a text by reflecting upon different readings of it.

HANDY HINT

Any text can be 'read', regardless of its mode/s of communication. Reading is the process of making meaning or developing an interpretation of a text, so the visual language of an image or the spoken language in a speech can also be 'read' for its meaning.

ACTIVITIES

10-minute activity

Brainstorm the multiple reasons why audiences might have different readings of a text.

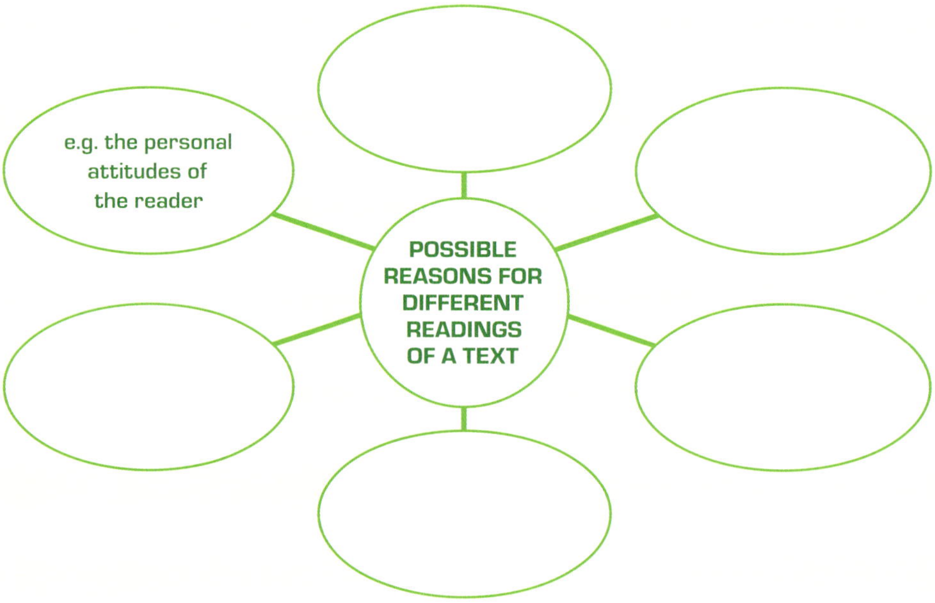

20-minute activity

Conduct an online search for reviews and analysis of a selected studied text, then note any points of difference between their interpretations of, or responses to, the text.

60-minute activity

With reference to one of your studied texts, write a full analytical response to Responding Practice Question 13. Your response should demonstrate your critical thinking skills.

Responding Practice Question 14

Explain how the assumptions that underpin a text might be challenged as a result of contextual influences.

HANDY HINT

An assumption is a belief or idea accepted as true without question or proof. The syllabus requires that you question the assumptions that underpin texts. This demands a critical reading, whereby you examine the assumptions a text's creator has made in constructing a representation or promoting a viewpoint.

10-minute activity

Deconstruct the key terms of the question according to:

command word/s: ______________________________

concept word/s: ______________________________

condition word/s: ______________________________

critical word/s: ______________________________

20-minute activity

Re-create the table below, then brainstorm a list of assumptions evident in one of your studied texts and the contextual factors that have resulted in these assumptions being questioned or challenged. An example is provided to get you started.

Text	Assumptions	Contextual factors
Nosedive	Mobile phone technology and social media interactions are detrimental to human relationships because they perpetuate social division and inauthentic interactions.	The circumstances of 2020 challenge this assumption because mobile phones and social media have played an integral role in maintaining human connections, despite the challenges of physical distance between people.

60-minute activity

With reference to one of your studied texts, write a full analytical response to Responding Practice Question 14. Your response should demonstrate your critical thinking skills.

Responding Practice Question 15

Show how your response to a studied text's central ideas has been shaped by its inclusions and/or emphases.

HANDY HINT You are essentially being asked to consider the creator's selection of detail in a text. Consider the specific content the creator/s have chosen to include and/or emphasise as important.

ACTIVITIES

10-minute activity

a Locate the syllabus bullet point that Responding Practice Question 15 corresponds to and write it in full in the space below.

____

____

b Now record definitions for the following terms in this syllabus point.

inclusions: ______________________________

____

emphases: ______________________________

____

omissions: ______________________________

____

marginalisations: ______________________________

____

20-minute activity

Create a marking guide for Responding Practice Question 15. Use the example provided on pages 95–6 as a model.

60-minute activity

With reference to one of your studied texts, write a full analytical response to Responding Practice Question 15. Your response should demonstrate your critical thinking skills.

Composing Practice

CHAPTER 4

This chapter addresses the demands of Section Three of the examination. It includes 15 different questions that provide opportunities to practise writing a range of texts in imaginative, interpretive and persuasive forms. In keeping with the style of previous Composing sections from past ATAR exams, some of the questions provided here include stimulus material in the form of visual prompts or quotes. A working time of 60 minutes is recommended for each of these practice questions, reflecting the demands of Section Three of the exam. In addition to these 15 Composing section practice questions, this chapter includes the following.

- A 10-minute activity accompanying each practice question provides scaffolded support to help decode the questions effectively and to plan responses to the questions.
- A 20-minute activity accompanying each practice question generally provides an opportunity to consider the question more closely, to produce a detailed plan and to write and/or reflect on part of a response, such as its exposition or its first page. Tasks provide guidance about how to effectively reflect a sense of audience, purpose and context within responses, as well as how to demonstrate a deep understanding of form and genre.
- Brief 'handy hints' accompany some of the questions that might present particular pitfalls; the hints will help you to properly deconstruct the questions so that you are able to respond to them appropriately.

WHAT TO EXPECT IN SECTION THREE

This is what you can expect to encounter in the Composing section.

- The questions will be designed to assess your understanding of syllabus concepts such as voice, genre or perspective, through their practical application within your response.

- You will almost certainly encounter questions that are different from those that you have addressed in class assessments. It is highly improbable that a piece of writing you have previously used or prepared will provide an adequate response to the new questions you will face in the exam.
- You will, however, be able to use the writing approaches that may have given you successful results before, such as control of language, structure and style appropriate to form. Work on the ability to adapt your writing skills to a wide range of questions and prompts.
- You will need to make decisions about which question to select and what form to use in your response. Although many candidates enter the examination with some sense of their strengths in terms of composing imaginative, interpretive or persuasive text types, there are still many forms available within each of these categories. For example, a persuasive text could take the form of a speech, a debate, an open letter, an opinion piece and so on.
- You will likely be given an opportunity to draw on your own experiences and/or knowledge of the world to create an original piece of writing.

TYPES OF QUESTIONS IN SECTION THREE

In this section you are required to compose a text in response to one out of a possible four or five questions. The Composing section questions often take the form of a stimulus prompt, topic or instruction. You may be asked to create a piece of writing that responds to an image or instruction, or which integrates or explores the ideas within a quote. Through a command word, the questions will direct you to respond in either an imaginative, interpretive or persuasive form. Sometimes you are permitted to make your own decision, as indicated by the phrase ‘in a form of your choice’. Composing section questions usually feature one or more syllabus concept words and phrases. As in the other sections, the Composing section questions are likely to include condition and critical words, explained on page 2.

Example Responding Question

Craft an imaginative text in which contrasting values are represented as the cause of conflict.

The most important considerations for the types of questions in this section are:

- recognising whether your response to a question needs to take an imaginative, interpretative or persuasive form, or a form of your own choice from among these options
- developing a good understanding of the specific forms that are accepted in these text categories, including the conventions they may use
- being able to correctly identify the specific syllabus concepts being assessed
- recognising the nuanced meanings of command, condition and critical words that may be designed to help differentiate between ineffective, effective and highly effective responses.

Given that the questions in this section are designed to help you demonstrate your writing skills, it is well worth practising the use of literary devices such as sensory imagery, figurative language and rhetoric. Learn how to confidently construct tone and voice, as well as how to structure various text forms.

The types of questions included in this section may require you to:

- understand the distinguishing features of imaginative, interpretive and persuasive text types
- demonstrate control of the specific generic conventions and the techniques associated with particular text forms, genres or styles of writing
- draw or reflect on your personal context, experiences, attitudes, values and perspectives
- use vocabulary, syntax, tone and punctuation in both conventional and potentially innovative ways for effect
- consider the relationship between syllabus concepts
- create two texts in response to the same question
- construct a particular voice, tone and style in your writing
- develop ideas for texts that are engaging, original or creative.

TOP TIPS FOR SECTION THREE

There are numerous strategies that can help you to improve your performance in Section Three of the examination. The tips outlined below include some advice for achieving success in this section.

- Select your question carefully, ensuring that you have identified and understood the syllabus concept/s it requires you to address. Base your decision on which question will best allow you to capitalise on your personal strengths; for example, some candidates feel greater confidence writing in persuasive forms than imaginative, and vice versa. Consider the forms you have previously produced successfully. *All* questions have a possible 30 marks available; no single question or form of response is privileged or preferred over another.
- Deconstruct the selected question carefully. Identify its command, concept, condition and critical words. Some candidates find it helpful to think of synonyms for some of the words in the question.
- Plan! This process is critical in terms of focusing your thoughts and providing you with a clear framework. A plan could include a plot diagram or a few dot points related to the intended audience, context, purpose, genre and/or form of your response.
- Make sure your response engages with all parts of the question or prompt. You could create a fabulous piece of writing, but unless it engages adequately with the question then you will not be able to achieve strong results.
- Structure your response appropriately, in a way suited to its form. This will often mean its physical appearance will be quite unlike your Responding analytical essay, with much more varied and flexible paragraphing.
- Use a title, and possibly a subtitle, to orientate the reader. These features are not only conventions of many forms of writing, they can also assist you to effectively indicate the genre, form, audience, purpose, subject matter and context of your piece.
- Demonstrate originality and embrace your own context and experiences as valid and authentic sources of inspiration.
- Aspects such as written expression and fluency are very important in this section. So, too, is the use of language that is typical of the form you are writing in. Show how you can use language for emotive, rhetorical or other effects.

PRACTICE QUESTIONS AND ACTIVITIES

This section contains a variety of practice questions and activities to develop your skills.

Composing Practice Question 1

Compose an imaginative text that explores the reason for the journey taken by the characters in this image.

10-minute activity

Brainstorm three suitable titles for an imaginative response to Composing Practice Question 1. You might also like to include a subtitle for each.

Title 1: ______________________________

Title 2: ______________________________

Title 3: ______________________________

20-minute activity

a Take 15 minutes to craft the opening page of an imaginative response to Composing Practice Question 1. Ensure that you start with a title!

b Compare the opening of your response with the Sample Marking Guide provided on pages 96–7.

60-minute activity

Write a complete response to Composing Practice Question 1. Your response should demonstrate your writing skills in a form appropriate to a specific audience, purpose and context.

Composing Practice Question 2

Create a text that interprets a real historical event from the perspective of someone who experienced it firsthand.

HANDY HINT Although the question doesn't use the specific words 'interpretive text', it can be assumed that a response should take this form, due to the requirement that the text 'interprets' a real historical event.

ACTIVITIES

10-minute activity

In the space below, compile a list of historical events you could use as inspiration for creating an interpretive text in response to Composing Practice Question 2.

Event 1: ______________________________

Event 2: ______________________________

Event 3: ______________________________

Event 4: ______________________________

Event 5: ______________________________

20-minute activity

Make notes under the following headings to plan a response to Composing Practice Question 2.

- historical event
- key facts known about the event
- identity of a selected person who experienced the event (name/role/profession etc.)
- viewpoint of the selected person related to the event
- contextual influences shaping the viewpoint of the selected person
- possible techniques used to interpret the event through the selected person's perspective (e.g. voice, type of language used, tone)

60-minute activity

Write a complete response to Composing Practice Question 2. Your response should demonstrate your writing skills in a form appropriate to a specific audience, purpose and context.

Composing Practice Question 3

'We who have means and a voice must use them to help those who have neither. Yet how can we help them if we don't even know about them?'

Create a persuasive text that explores the idea expressed in this quote.

10-minute activity

In the space below, compile a list of rhetorical devices and techniques you could use in a persuasive text that responds to Composing Practice Question 3.

20-minute activity

In the spaces below, draft a plan for a persuasive text that responds to Composing Practice Question 3.

Form of persuasive text (e.g. speech, opinion piece):	Target audience:	Context of situation (where and when would the text be read/received?):
Conventions of form:	Specific purpose of text:	Who are the 'we' and 'them' in the prompt?

60-minute activity

Write a complete response to Composing Practice Question 3. Your response should demonstrate your writing skills in a form appropriate to a specific audience, purpose and context.

Composing Practice Question 4

In a form of your choice, create a text that explores the role of humour in contemporary society.

ACTIVITIES

10-minute activity

Start planning your response to Composing Practice Question 4 in the diagram below, by noting forms in which humour is expressed in contemporary society.

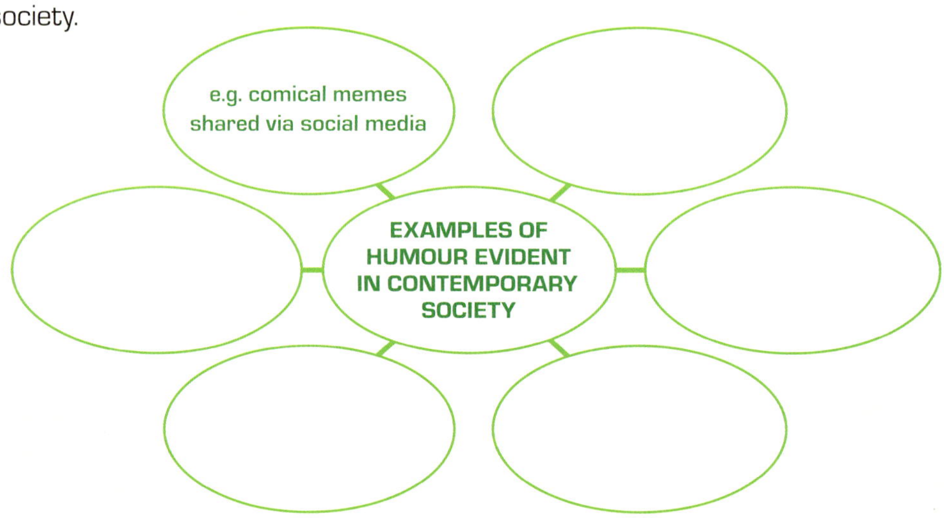

20-minute activity

a In the table below, list a range of ideas for each text type in response to Composing Practice Question 4.

Imaginative text ideas	Interpretive text ideas	Persuasive text ideas

b Now select one of these ideas and write the opening of a text.

60-minute activity

Write a complete response to Composing Practice Question 4. Your response should demonstrate your writing skills in a form appropriate to a specific audience, purpose and context.

Composing Practice Question 5

Craft an imaginative text in a particular genre which uses the following sentence as its opening line:

It was hardly worth looking back now, but she directed a cursory glance over her shoulder anyway, just to make sure.

10-minute activity

In the space below, make a list of conventions and techniques associated with imaginative forms of writing. Consider grouping the conventions and techniques under separate headings that indicate the specific genre they are associated with.

20-minute activity

a Spend 10 minutes writing the opening to an imaginative text in response to Composing Practice Question 5.

b Use an additional five minutes to highlight **one** of the following elements in your response:

- adjectives
- verbs
- adverbs

c Now spend another five minutes substituting these highlighted words with more interesting or precise choices. You might find it helpful to use a dictionary or a thesaurus.

60-minute activity

Write a complete response to Composing Practice Question 5. Your response should demonstrate your writing skills in a form appropriate to a specific audience, purpose and context.

Composing Practice Question 6

Compose an interpretive text that engages with an idea represented by this image.

ACTIVITIES

10-minute activity

Summarise two different ideas represented in the image, using complete sentences.

1 ____

____

____

2 ____

____

____

20-minute activity

Produce a marking guide to accompany Composing Practice Question 6. Use the example provided on pages 96–7 as a model.

60-minute activity

Write a complete response to Composing Practice Question 6. Your response should demonstrate your writing skills in a form appropriate to a specific audience, purpose and context.

Composing Practice Question 7

Compose two persuasive texts that present contrasting perspectives on the same moment of controversy.

HANDY HINT

The critical word 'moment' indicates that the focus should be on a very limited duration of time, even though the controversy generated may be prolonged. Examples could include an event, a comment or a decision, or an action deemed to be polarising and therefore 'controversial'.

10-minute activity

Complete the following Venn diagram to plan a response to Composing Practice Question 7. Choose a controversy you are familiar with.

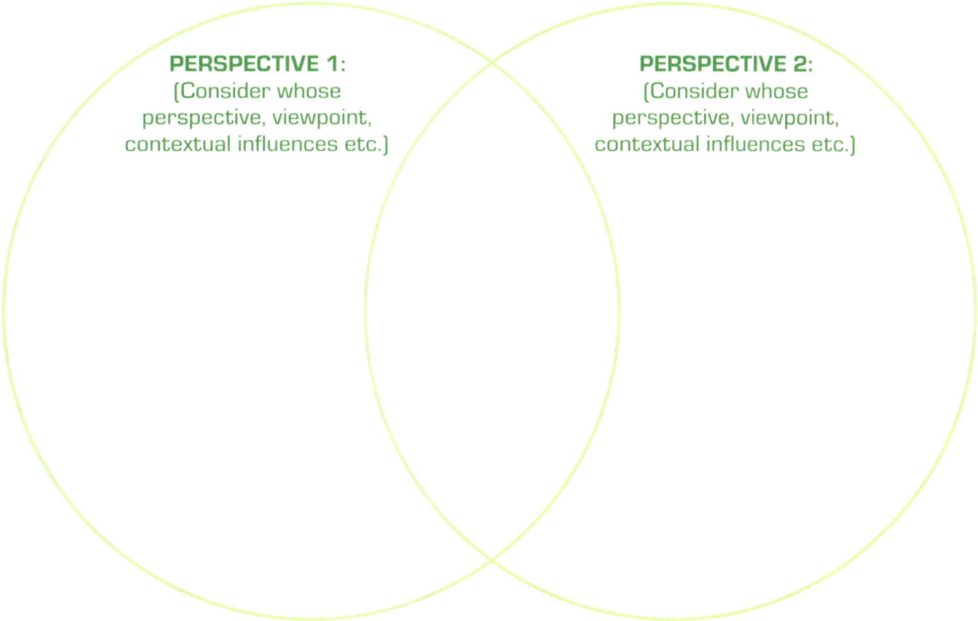

20-minute activity

Select a moment of controversy, and find at least two pieces of evidence online that highlight the controversial nature of the moment and the contrasting viewpoints it has generated. Evidence could include a letter to the editor, an opinion piece, a satirical cartoon, a persuasive speech or a review.

60-minute activity

Write a complete response to Composing Practice Question 7. Your response should demonstrate your writing skills in a form appropriate to a specific audience, purpose and context.

Composing Practice Question 8

In a form of your choice, create a text that seeks to question a common societal assumption.

HANDY HINT The assumption selected should be one that is common or prevalent in a particular society or social group. Provide evidence to support the contention that the assumption is a 'common' one.

ACTIVITIES

10-minute activity

In the space below, compile a list of assumptions. These could be the assumptions in your studied texts, assumptions you observe broadly in society, or the assumptions associated with certain groups or cultural contexts. An example has been given for you.

- Working hard will lead to success.
- ______________________________
- ______________________________
- ______________________________
- ______________________________
- ______________________________

20-minute activity

Use Composing Practice Question 8 as the stimulus for a class or study group discussion about the concept of 'assumptions'. During the discussion:

- identify the assumptions that underpin your studied text/s
- explain one of your own assumptions and whether you believe it is widespread, or 'common' in society
- compile a list of ideas for each possible text type in response to Composing Practice Question 8.

60-minute activity

Write a complete response to Composing Practice Question 8. Your response should demonstrate your writing skills in a form appropriate to a specific audience, purpose and context.

Composing Practice Question 9

Craft an imaginative text of a specific genre that begins and ends in this setting.

ACTIVITIES

10-minute activity

Describe this setting using each of the following types of sensory imagery. Write one sentence for each.

Visual (sight): ______________________________

____

Olfactory (smell): ______________________________

____

Tactile (touch): ______________________________

____

Auditory (sound): ______________________________

____

Kinaesthetic (movement): ______________________________

____

Gustatory (taste): ______________________________

____

Organic (emotion/personal experiences e.g. nostalgia, pain, thirst):

____

____

Thermal (temperature): ______________________________

____

20-minute activity

Using the various types of sensory imagery listed above, create the exposition to an imaginative text that responds to Composing Practice Question 9.

60-minute activity

Write a complete response to Composing Practice Question 9. Your response should demonstrate your writing skills in a form appropriate to a specific audience, purpose and context.

Composing Practice Question 10

Create an interpretive text in which you reflect closely on an event that has contributed to one of your personal values.

HANDY HINT Values are different from attitudes. Locate the definitions of both 'values' and 'attitudes' if necessary.

10-minute activity

Compile a list of 10 personal values, then rank them from most important (1) to least important (10) to you.

20-minute activity

Answer the following questions in full sentences.

- **a** What are your three most important personal values?
- **b** Which aspects of your personal context have contributed to these values? Consider your age, gender, experiences, upbringing, peer group, cultural identity etc.
- **c** Explain how one of these values has been either strengthened or challenged by one of your experiences.
- **d** Compare your current values with those you prioritised five years ago, considering whether they have changed or remained the same. Explain why you think this is.
- **e** Explain why you think someone else may have different personal values from you.

60-minute activity

Write a complete response to Composing Practice Question 10. Your response should demonstrate your writing skills in a form appropriate to a specific audience, purpose and context.

Composing Practice Question 11

Create a sustained persuasive argument which either supports or challenges the idea embedded in the following statement:

"Nothing is so painful to the human mind as a great and sudden change."

ACTIVITIES

10-minute activity

a In the space below, define the term 'sustained'.

b List some forms of writing that could allow you to create a sustained persuasive argument.

c Select one of these forms and make a list of conventions and techniques typical of this form.

20-minute activity

a Re-create the table below and use it to brainstorm the arguments for and against the statement in Composing Practice Question 11. Consider a specific issue, topic or event that you could connect to the statement.

"Nothing is so painful to the human mind as a great and sudden change."	
FOR (supports idea)	**AGAINST** (challenges idea)

b Now use the points identified as a stimulus for a class debate or discussion.

60-minute activity

Write a complete response to Composing Practice Question 11. Your response should demonstrate your writing skills in a form appropriate to a specific audience, purpose and context.

Composing Practice Question 12

In a form of your choice, compose a text that explores an idea created by your interpretation of this scene.

ACTIVITIES

10-minute activity

Annotate the text, thinking about the numerous ideas it generates. Select one of these ideas and write it in the space below as a full sentence.

___

___

20-minute activity

Craft the opening page of a response to Composing Question 12.

60-minute activity

Write a complete response to Composing Practice Question 12. Your response should demonstrate your writing skills in a form appropriate to a specific audience, purpose and context.

Composing Practice Question 13

Compose an imaginative text in which the voice of its central character evokes empathy from readers.

ACTIVITIES

10-minute activity

a Record definitions for the following terms in the space provided below.

Sympathy: ______________________________

____

Empathy: ______________________________

____

b Now write a sentence explaining the difference between sympathy and empathy in your own words.

____

____

20-minute activity

a Re-create the table below and add definitions of the common structural techniques used in imaginative texts.

Structural technique	Definition
Flashback	
Foreshadowing	
Unexpected twist	
Circular narrative	
Language patterns	
Recurring symbol or motif	

b Now identify which of these techniques have been used in one of your studied imaginative texts and record a specific example of each.

60-minute activity

Write a complete response to Composing Practice Question 13. Your response should demonstrate your writing skills in a form appropriate to a specific audience, purpose and context.

Composing Practice Question 14

Use the following quotation as a headline or title for an interpretive text:

"We can't blame the technology, when we make the mistakes."

HANDY HINT Remember that the main purpose of an interpretive text is to explain and interpret the subject matter rather than persuade an audience to accept the viewpoint proposed.

ACTIVITIES

10-minute activity

Using Composing Practice Question 14, think of three possible approaches you could take in an interpretive text that uses the quotation as a headline or title. It might be useful to focus on a specific aspect or example of technology.

Approach 1: ______________________________

____

Approach 2: ______________________________

____

Approach 3: ______________________________

____

20-minute activity

Create an opening to your interpretive text that includes one of the following techniques:

- an engaging anecdote
- a humorous tale
- a case study or example
- evidence from a research study
- an interesting fact or statistic
- an expert opinion

60-minute activity

Write a complete response to Composing Practice Question 14. Your response should demonstrate your writing skills in a form appropriate to a specific audience, purpose and context.

Composing Practice Question 15

Compose two persuasive texts that present contrasting viewpoints on the same issue.

ACTIVITIES

10-minute activity

Plan the following aspects (the GAPPS) of your two responses to Composing Practice Question 15.

GAPPS	Explanation	Text 1	Text 2
Genre	Which genre or form will you write each text in?		
Audience	Who is the specific audience for your text?		
Purpose	What is the primary purpose of your text?		
Persona	What credible persona will you adopt to write the text?		
Situational context	Where and when, exactly, would the text be received?		

20-minute activity

a Complete the 10-minute activity above.

b Now create a title for, and the opening lines of, a text that seeks to orient the reader or marker, by filling in these GAPPS.

c Using a different colour for each aspect, highlight where you have revealed the genre or form, audience, purpose, persona and situational context of your text in its title or its first few lines.

60-minute activity

Write a complete response to Composing Practice Question 15. Your response should demonstrate your writing skills in a form appropriate to a specific audience, purpose and context.

Sample Marking Guides

CHAPTER 5

This chapter contains holistic marking guides for responses to sample questions for each of the three sections of the examination. The marking guides indicate the qualities of effective responses. In addition to these guides, it is strongly recommended that you familiarise yourself with the marking keys applied to past ATAR examinations (available on the SCSA website). These offer useful summaries of the principles and criteria relevant to each exam section.

SECTION ONE: COMPREHENDING

This Sample Marking Guide provides examples of what a response to Comprehending Practice Question 1 (page 15; Text 1 begins on page 14) could include and be rewarded for. Emphasis is placed on the effectiveness of the response in terms of demonstrating comprehension and analytical skills. This marking guide should not be considered an exhaustive list; other insightful comments about the text may also be evident in responses.

Comprehending Practice Question 1 (15 marks)

Analyse the relationship between setting and character in Text 1.

Structure and written expression

- A key discriminator is the extent to which the candidate's response is expressed in a clear, concise and logically organised manner.
- Stronger responses will present insightful comments fluently and succinctly in approximately 200–300 words.
- Stronger responses will use correct metalanguage and vocabulary appropriate to the question.

Content

- Stronger analyses may focus on the way the character engages or interacts with the setting, is affected or influenced by the setting, expresses her curiosity about the setting, or observes the juxtaposition between the human experience of ageing and the building in its setting.
- Stronger analysis may focus on specific aspects of characterisation, such as actions, thoughts and attitudes, as well as features that establish the temporal and/or spatial setting.
- A key discriminator between effective and less effective responses could be the extent to which candidates examine, in an integrated manner, the relationship between the narrative conventions.

Supporting evidence

Supporting evidence may include analysis of:

- the text, using brief, appropriately selected and well-integrated quotes and/or paraphrasing to support points
- the use of sensory imagery to highlight the impact of the setting on the character (e.g. kinaesthetic description of the building's bricks that 'jut' into the character's back, olfactory imagery of the 'smell of gunpowder', which fills the air when she picks up the paper)
- the use of adjectives such as the 'rusted' steel of the setting's interior, connotative verbs including the 'canting and creaking' of the sign, and the noun 'a ruin', suggesting the setting's enduring state of disrepair and neglect, which is contrasted with the fate of people
- figurative language devices, such as assonance to describe the way 'new life drifts in on breezes and seeds', personification to describe the 'yawning openings' of the walls, and metaphor and alliteration to describe the 'concrete crumbs' of the building
- the way the character is influenced by the setting to reflect on the death of people (e.g. the death of a building is 'more a rebirth, Lou thinks')
- the way the character considers and contemplates her surroundings as she physically engages with part of it ('An asinine gesture, she thinks', as she rubs her wrist on a canister).

SECTION TWO: RESPONDING

This marking guide provides examples of what an answer to Responding Practice Question 1 (page 58) could include and be rewarded for. Emphasis is placed on the effectiveness of the response in terms of demonstrating critical thinking and analytical skills with reference to a studied text. This marking guide should not be considered an exhaustive list; other possible points of analysis about the selected studied text/s related to the question may also be evident in responses.

Responding Practice Question 1 (40 marks)

Analyse how the language, structural and stylistic choices evident within one text have influenced your response to it.

Structure and written expression

- A key discriminator is the extent to which the response is expressed in a clear and logically organised manner; stronger responses will provide insightful analysis, presented fluently, to sustain a central argument. The use of personal voice is appropriate to the question.
- Strong responses will use correct metalanguage and vocabulary appropriate to the question.

Content

- A key discriminator is the extent to which the response engages deeply and critically with the question, demonstrating an understanding that the command word 'analyse' requires careful consideration of the component parts of a text, including identifying patterns and relationships, extracting meanings and implications, and identifying the effects of particular choices.
- More insightful analysis will focus on the effects of language, structural and stylistic choices in influencing a specific personal response to the text; the response/s should be specifically identified (e.g. shock, discomfort, curiosity, empathy, compassion, confusion, motivation).
- Analysis may discuss multiple responses linked to the different choices, or focus on one central response shaped by the cumulative effect of the choices.
- Analysis may examine the relationship between the language, structural and stylistic choices or examine them separately; responses may recognise that there can be overlap between language, structural and stylistic choices.

- Stronger analysis might acknowledge that the text's creator has purposefully made specific language, structural and stylistic 'choices'; a high-quality response will clearly differentiate 'features' from 'choices'.
- Candidates may argue that the choices had little or limited influence on their response so long as this contention is well justified.

Supporting evidence

Supporting evidence may include analysis of:

- brief, appropriately selected and well-integrated textual evidence and/or quotes
- the influence and effects of specific language choices made by the text's creator/s, such as the use of particular filmic or visual language and the use of figurative language, connotative language or rhetorical devices
- the influence and effects of specific structural choices made by the text's creator/s, such as the approach taken to the sequencing and organisation of content, including the use of chapters, paragraphs, foreshadowing, flashbacks and syntax
- the influence and effects of specific stylistic choices made by the text's creator/s, such as narrative point of view, voice, tone, lexical choice and colour scheme
- the connection between the textual features and the candidate's personal responses; this will be clearly established and sustained in a strong response.

SECTION THREE: COMPOSING

This marking guide provides examples of what a response to Composing Practice Question 1 (page 77) could include and be rewarded for. Emphasis is placed on the effectiveness of the response in terms of demonstrating composing skills through control of language and generic conventions appropriate to a particular form, purpose and audience. This marking guide should not be considered an exhaustive list; other possible features may also be evident in responses.

Composing Practice Question 1 (30 marks)

Compose an imaginative text that explores the reason for the journey taken by the characters in this image.

Structure and written expression

- A key discriminator is the extent to which the response is expressed in a clear, fluent and logically organised manner.
- Stronger responses will use vocabulary and language choices appropriate to the requirement that responses be 'imaginative' in form.

Content

- A key discriminator is the extent to which the response engages with the stimulus prompt in the question, which indicates that the response should focus on one reason for the characters' journey. The question implies that the characters featured in the image have the same reason for their journey and share a clear sense of destination. Their reason could be revealed overtly, or subtly implied through such aspects as their dialogue, actions, interactions with each other and the setting; the narrative point of view; or other features of the response.
- The response should establish a clear connection to the ideas contained within the image prompt, perhaps through development of its generic conventions, such as characterisation and narrative structure.
- Stronger responses will demonstrate an understanding that the primary purpose of imaginative texts is to use literary elements in order to entertain or provoke thought in an audience; the degree to which the response achieves this can be a key factor in judging the quality of responses.
- Imaginative responses could take a number of forms, including a short story or a play script. Stronger responses will convey a clearly recognisable form and genre. The degree to which the response demonstrates mastery of the relevant generic conventions will determine the quality of the response.
- Stronger responses will engage fully with the command word 'compose', which directs students to write purposefully using language, structural, stylistic and generic features for effect; this may involve the use of such features as sensory imagery, figurative language, syntax, structural devices, voice and tone.
- Stronger responses will reflect competence in writing creatively and descriptively in order to shape reader responses.
- While the 'journey' referred to in the prompt is open to interpretation, it should take into account the setting conveyed by the image (e.g. railway track bordered by vegetation, lack of other characters or urban development).

ABOUT THE AUTHORS

Leanne Bondin

Leanne has been an English teacher for more than twenty years in Queensland and Western Australian secondary schools. She co-compiled several recent editions of the *Good Answers* study guides produced by ETAWA and has contributed to a number of other ATAR English examination-related resources as a writer or reviewer. Leanne has almost fifteen years of experience as a WACE and ATAR marker and holds a Bachelor of Education (Hons) and a Masters of Education (Contemporary Literacies). She has presented ATAR English masterclasses and revision seminars, lectures at the Curtin University English and Literature conferences, and other professional learning sessions for English teachers. Leanne currently works at Rossmoyne Senior High School as the Assistant Head of Learning Area – English, where she coordinates the Year 12 ATAR English course. Leanne has a particular interest in curriculum, assessment and resource design, as well as assessment feedback practices.

Louise Pettigrew

Louise has been an English and Literature teacher in the Catholic sector of education for more than ten years. She holds a Bachelor of Arts, with a major in English Literature, from Curtin University and a Dip Ed from the University of Western Australia. Louise has co-compiled the *Good Answers* study guide produced by ETAWA. She is an experienced Year 12 ATAR English and Literature teacher, as well as an experienced WACE marker. She currently works at Sacred Heart College in Sorrento and is the Year 12 English ATAR program and assessment coordinator. Louise is passionate about engaging students in a love of literature and developing programs that assist students in developing both their analytical and creative writing skills.

ACKNOWLEDGEMENTS

The publishers are grateful to the following individuals and organisations for permission to reproduce copyright material.

Articles and book excerpts

Michelle Johnston and UWA Publishing for the excerpt from *Dustfall*; Zachary Bruce and *ABC News* for the excerpt from 'WA town of Ballidu is "doing its own thing" with contemporary art', reproduced by permission of the Australian Broadcasting Corporation – Library Sales, Zachary Bruce © 2020 ABC; Nicole Hasham and *The Conversation* for the excerpt from 'Making sense of Australia's bushfire crisis – and listening to the answers'; EL Marriott for the excerpt from 'Purple Little Hearts'; Tim Winton and Penguin Australia for the excerpt from *Island Home*; Dr David Smith for the autobiographical reflection; Peter FitzSimons and *The Sydney Morning Herald* for the excerpt from '"It's freaking hopeless": why the Health Star Rating System has to go'; Allanah Hunt and *Griffith Review* for the excerpt from 'Spectrums'; Antony Funnell and *ABC Radio National* for the excerpt from 'Myths of the Near Future', reproduced by permission of the Australian Broadcasting Corporation – Library Sales, © 2015 ABC; Ali O'Reilly and *McSweeney's* for the excerpt from 'An Open Letter To The Phrase "Positive Vibes Only"'; Neil Grant and Allen & Unwin for the extract from *The Honeyman and the Hunter*, first published in Sydney, 2019; Andrew Bain, *Traveller* and traveller.com.au for the excerpt from 'Cruising The Kimberly and Horizontal Falls: Australia's most unusual natural wonder', published by *The Sydney Morning Herald* and *The Age*; Julia Gillard for the excerpt from 'International Women's Day Breakfast' under Creative Commons 4.0, https://creativecommons.org/licenses/by/4.0/legalcode.

Images

Stuart Franklin and Magnum Photos for 'Manchester. Moss Side Estate'; Peggy Sirota for the advertisement for Patek Phillippe; Charles Burns and Penguin Random House UK for the excerpt from *Black Hole #5*; Dan Nelson for the image of India 2013; *New Scientist* for the image of the cover of *New Scientist* issue 3049; SBS for the greyscale version of a still from the SBS television miniseries *The Hunting* (2019); Alamy for the posters for *The Adventures of Priscilla, Queen of the Desert* and *On the Basis of Sex*; Joanna Delalande and *The West Australian* for the front-page image accompanying the article 'Heroes Welcome'; Dan Nelson for the image of the fruit seller.

Other images from Pixabay and Pexels.